GOD OF
Comfort
GOD OF
Love

GOD OF Comfort GOD OF Love

Spencer J. Condie

BOOKCRAFT
Salt Lake City, Utah

Library of Congress Catalog Card Number 98-70869
ISBN 1-57008-416-5

First Printing, 1998

Printed in the United States of America

To my parents, Spencer and Josie,
who have provided comfort and love
to so many others for many years,
and to all their good neighbors who now
provide comfort and love to them.

CONTENTS

ACKNOWLEDGMENTS

THERE ARE COUNTLESS FAITHFUL SAINTS whose lives provide patterns of hope and courage in the face of seemingly insurmountable obstacles. Some of their experiences are included in this volume, and I am grateful to them for their enduring examples and trust that others will find them to be a source of comfort and strength. Some of their most courageous actions have been to forgive those who often least deserve forgiveness, thus reflecting the depth of their testimonies of the atonement of Jesus Christ. I am also grateful to living prophets, seers, and revelators who continually extend the Savior's comfort and His love.

This book would not have seen the light of day without the caring critique of Stefanie Condie, the meticulous editing of George Bickerstaff, and the sustaining encouragement of Cory Maxwell.

This is not an official publication of The Church of Jesus Christ of Latter-day Saints, and, notwithstanding the assistance of others, I alone bear the responsibility for all of its shortcomings.

PART ONE

God of Comfort

And he came to Nazareth, where he had been brought up:
and, as his custom was, he went into the synagogue on
the sabbath day, and stood up for to read.

And there was delivered unto him
the book of the prophet Esaias.
And when he had opened the book,
he found the place where it was written,

The Spirit of the Lord is upon me, because he
hath anointed me to preach the gospel to the poor;
he hath sent me to heal the brokenhearted,
to preach deliverance to the captives,
and recovering of sight to the blind,
to set at liberty them that are bruised,

To preach the acceptable year of the Lord.

And he closed the book, and he gave it again to the minister,
and sat down. And the eyes of all them that were
in the synagogue were fastened on him.

And he began to say unto them,
This day is this scripture fulfilled in your ears.

—LUKE 4:16–21

ONE

I Will Not Leave You Comfortless

THE CHAPEL WAS FILLED TO OVERFLOWING, yet an uncommon silence prevailed, punctuated by occasional sniffles from members of the congregation. This was a funeral service that everyone will long remember. Earlier in the week the young husband had taken his thirty-year-old wife to the hospital, where she gave birth to a beautiful, healthy baby girl. Now their family had two boys and two girls and everything was right with the world. Filled with gratitude for his many blessings, the young father kissed his wife goodbye in the hospital and returned home to collect his three other little ones from the neighbors to tell them the great news: they had a new baby sister!

That evening their home was filled with joy and great anticipation. In just another day or two Mommy would be coming home with a new baby. But alas, very early the next morning the young father was awakened by an alarming phone call from the hospital. The voice on the other end of the line urged him to come to the hospital immediately. He prevailed upon some neighbors to watch his sleeping children while he rushed to the hospital. As he reached the obstetrics ward and scanned the facial expressions of the doctor and the nurses he immediately

3

sensed that something had gone very wrong. "We're sorry to inform you," the doctor said somewhat haltingly, "that some time this evening your wife evidently passed a blood clot which impaired her circulation, and she passed away. We're very, very sorry."

Just a few short hours previously the young father had experienced joy unbounded, but now his anguish was unbearable. In a daze he returned home to disclose the heart-breaking news to his children, the oldest of whom was seven, and to tell his wife's parents and his own parents that tragedy had struck their little family overnight.

Now, nearly a week later, loved ones, neighbors, friends, and associates were gathered in stunned silence to pay their last respects to a valiant young mother in Zion and to express their love and support to her grieving husband and their children, who were almost too young even to comprehend the consequences of their mother's untimely death. Though most members in the congregation had firm testimonies of the resurrection and a confirmation of the sealing power, there were still expressions of wonderment as to why a loving Father in Heaven would allow such a tragedy to occur. Some friends and neighbors even expressed a certain bitterness that God would permit four little children to lose their mother so suddenly.

The invocation to the meeting invited the Spirit of the Lord into the funeral service and the speakers spoke words of comfort based upon the doctrinal promises of the scriptures, but still a lingering feeling of disquietude prevailed. Although it was extremely difficult for her to sing, a talented and spiritually sensitive soprano sang a beautiful song of comfort, but she failed to disguise her inner feelings of grief. After the final speaker drew to a close the bishop prepared to conclude the meeting. But then, to the surprise of all, this young father rose from his seat at the front of the congregation, and with reverential majesty he came to the pulpit and asked for the opportunity briefly to address the congregation of mourners.

With complete composure and a voice that was strong and unfaltering he said: "When I came home from the hospital after they told me my wife had suddenly passed away, I thought my heart was going to break. I didn't know how I could stand it. What was I going to do to rear these three little children and a brand new baby? The anguish and despair were so great, I did not think I could last another hour. But then I went into the bedroom and knelt in prayer and pleaded with my Father in Heaven for a measure of peace and comfort. And the comfort came. I was filled with the Spirit, and this calm and peaceful Spirit has been with me ever since. I know that things will work out and everything will be all right. Don't worry about us. We're going to be just fine." He concluded with an expression of gratitude for all his blessings and for the love he and his family had been shown by members of the ward.

The heavy spirit that had prevailed over the congregation was lifted in a perceptible way, and what had begun as a dreary, soul-wrenching, hankie-drenching experience became a pentacostal event with a wonderful, rich outpouring of the Spirit. The Saints returned to their homes comforted. Each had claimed the Savior's promise: "I will not leave you comfortless" (John 14:18).

Refusing to Be Comforted

As strange as it may seem, not everyone is willing to be comforted, at least during the initial stages of grief, disappointment, anguish, or fear. After Joseph's older brothers sold him to the Midianite merchants bound for Egypt, they dipped his coat of many colors in goat's blood and returned home, where they handed the coat to their father, Jacob, who immediately inferred that Joseph had been killed by a wild beast. Although his family members sought to comfort their grief-stricken father in his supposed hour of bereavement, Jacob "refused to be comforted" (Genesis 37:35). This is one of the saddest expressions in all of holy writ—the refusal to be comforted—especially in light of the Apostle Paul's reference to our accessibility to "the God of all comfort; who comforteth us in all our tribulation" (2 Corinthians 1:3–4).

Following the birth of Jesus, when King Herod ordered that all the children in Bethlehem and its surrounds "from two years and under" were to be slain, the grieving mothers of those precious infants fulfilled Jeremiah's prophecy of a time when there would be "lamentation, and weeping, and great mourning, Rachel weeping for her children, and would not be comforted." (Matthew 2:16–18; Jeremiah 31:15.)

Another case of unrelenting anguish is found in the concluding chapter of Ether, which records the annihilation of the entire Jaredite nation. Coriantumr was a prominent man of war who had led his military forces into numerous battles in which nearly two million of his people had been slain by the sword (see Ether 15:1–2). When he finally realized the futility of warfare, "He began to repent of the evil which he had done; he began to remember the words which had been spoken by the mouth of all the prophets, and he saw them that they were fulfilled thus far, every whit; and his soul mourned and refused to be comforted" (Ether 15:3).

Among the most heart-rending encounters we experience are discussions with individuals who have become weary and worn down by the countless trials and tribulations in their lives and who have begun to lose hope and not infrequently refuse to be comforted. These good people include a married couple who suddenly lose a young child to an acute illness, a lovely woman who has married a suitable man in good faith and is devastated to learn that he has been unfaithful to her, and an elderly couple who trust their life savings to an unscrupulous friend who absconds with all their retirement funds. There is also the young woman who repeatedly retrieves painful memories of abuse as a child, and the husband whose wife is killed in an automobile accident caused by a drunken driver. Still others who are at least temporarily bereft of comfort are the parents of a son who refuses to serve a mission, or parents who grieve over a son sent home early from his mission. Others in dire need of comfort are the parents whose married daughters are unable to bear children. Their anguish is matched by other parents whose fourteen-year-old daughter has recently borne a child out of wedlock. All of these persons, at least initially, may refuse to be comforted. Faith and hope may begin to dwindle as they perhaps forget that "men are that they might have joy" (2 Nephi 2:25).

The Lord reassured the ancient Israelites that he had refined them and "chosen [them] in the furnace of affliction" (Isaiah 48:10; see also 1 Nephi 20:10). Affliction, trials, and tribulation are part and parcel of our mortal probation, which includes an opposition in *all* things, and Father Lehi's promise to his young son, Jacob, holds true for each of us: notwithstanding our "afflictions and much sorrow . . . [God] shall consecrate [our] afflictions for [our] gain." (2 Nephi 2:1–2.)

Elder James E. Faust has promised that "out of the refiner's fire can come a glorious deliverance. It can be a noble and lasting rebirth. The price to become acquainted with God will have been paid. There can come a sacred peace. There will be a reawakening of dormant, inner resources. A comfortable cloak of righteousness will be drawn around us to protect us and to keep us warm spiritually. Self-pity will vanish as our blessings are counted." (James E. Faust, "The Refiner's Fire," *Ensign*, May 1979, p. 57.)

Loss of a Loved One

One of the greatest sources of anguish and affliction in our lives comes from the loss of something extremely valuable. Families who abruptly lose their homes through fire, flood, or tornado are temporarily devastated by the loss. The sudden loss of employment after years of loyal service can also be devastating to one's sense of self-worth, and the distress can be compounded by fears of an unpredictable financial future. But an even greater source of anguish in this world can be the despair consequential to the death of a loved one. Feelings of helplessness and hopelessness are compounded when the death is very sudden and especially when the recipient of the news is not rooted and settled in a testimony of the resurrection and life hereafter and the eternal promises inherent in temple ordinances. As one father put it after having retrieved his little daughter from the irrigation culvert in which she had drowned: "Now is not the time to get a testimony of the resurrection. If you don't have a testimony now, it's a little late to get one." His statement underscored the significance of the Lord's comforting promise that "they who have sought me early shall find rest to their souls" (D&C 54:10).

Nevertheless there are many people in the world who are forced to deal with the death of a loved one despite their lack of faith. Such a person is Alison Irvine, mother of Ross, a five-year-old boy who was killed by a crazed gunman along with his teacher and fifteen other children in the gymnasium of the Dunblane Primary School in Scotland on March 13, 1996. By her own admission, Alison *refuses to be comforted.*

Approaching the anniversary of her little boy's death, Alison said: "I'm not religious. I've had no comfort from all that. We were referred to a psychologist who is an expert in bereavement counselling, and we went a few weeks. Ian [my husband] still goes. It helps him. I don't [go]. I prefer to deal with it myself. . . . I got the impression that the psychologist felt that I should have been coming along faster. But the way I was raised was to have a stiff upper lip, put on a brave face. . . . There seems no future to us as a family, when one of us has gone. You wonder how you can manage. There's such a wide range of emotions. Sometimes you feel violent anger. Sometimes it's suicidal tendencies. You keep going because you have to go on—or take a decision not to. You don't think too far ahead. Grief is a very personal thing." (Magnus Linklater, "Dunblane Remembered," *The Times*, London, February 24, 1997, p. 17.) Our hearts go out to Alison and Ian Irvine, but the peace and comfort they need is, in the words of the Savior, "not as the world giveth" (John 14:27), but rather the peace which the God of all comfort can give, and this requires that we believe in Him and claim His promises.

Comfort as the World Giveth

The limitations of comfort provided by the methods of the world were addressed by Yvonne McEwen, a British expert in victim counseling who holds five international professorships. Professor McEwen was a consultant following the Pan American airplane explosion over Lockerbie, Scotland, and she also consulted with victims of terrorism in Northern Ireland, and in the United States following the bombing of the Alfred P. Murrah Federal Building in Oklahoma City.

After years of observing individual reactions to various disasters, Professor McEwen has concluded that "Swamping trauma victims with teams of professional counselors often creates more problems than it solves. . . . They don't need their psyches invaded. What they need is honest information about what is going on. They need to make their own decisions. . . . We need to listen to what they want and if they don't want counseling then that is fine. People like themselves better when they work something out for themselves. . . ." (Gillian Bowditch, "Disaster Specialist Attacks 'Monster' of Trauma Counseling," *The Times*, London, Wednesday, January 29, 1997, p. 6.)

The late Martin B. Hickman once gave me some valuable insight into the comfort "as the world giveth" reflected in the popular television series MASH, a sitcom about a medical and surgical headquarters unit during the Korean War. Brother Hickman recounted that one of the prominent members of the

army unit was a bespectacled chaplain with an Irish surname
and a high squeaky voice. He was a jovial fellow who was loved
and appreciated by all as he provided comic relief during the
antics of the doctors and nurses and staff. But when one of the
doctors or patients had to deal with an acute emotional problem or a spiritual crisis in their lives resulting from the stress of
the war, the *chaplain* was ignored and the *psychiatrist* was called
in from a neighboring medical unit to resolve the emotional
trauma. The chaplain's task was to conduct religious services,
but the psychiatrist was the first choice for relief from the cares
of the world and the troubles of the soul.

Peace Not as the World Giveth

In the Book of Mormon, Zeezrom "was a man who was expert in the devices of the devil," who cleverly sought to resist
the teachings and testimonies of Amulek and Alma. However,
with the passage of time Zeezrom experienced "a burning fever;
and his mind also was exceedingly sore because of his iniquities." Unlike Shakespeare's Macbeth, who pressed his physician
for some kind of remedy that would relieve himself and his wife
from the excruciating guilt of their evil deeds, Zeezrom sought
help from Alma and Amulek, who held the priesthood of God,
and implored them "that they would heal him." He indicated
that, though he had previously resisted their testimonies, he
now believed their words and he believed in the redemption of
Jesus Christ. Alma then proceeded to invoke a blessing upon
him and he was healed and leaped to his feet. The spiritual
healing and comfort continued as Alma baptized him and as he
preached to the people and accompanied Alma, Amulek, and
three of the four sons of Mosiah on a mission to the Zoramites
(Alma 11:21–46; 12:1–8; 15:3–12; 31:5–6). Zeezrom had received comfort not as the world giveth.

Numerous faithful members of the Church are psychiatrists
and clinical psychologists and professionally trained counselors,

men and women of integrity and faith who render competent and helpful service to their clientele. But even they would concur that in times of certain spiritual crises the Comforter can engender a peace "not as the world giveth," but a peace "which passeth all understanding" (Phillipians 4:7). The God of all comfort will come to our aid as the Savior promised His disciples of old; and as the Old Testament prophesied, He will "wipe away tears from off all faces" (Isaiah 25:8).

Enoch Rejoiced

One of the most righteous men to walk the earth was the ancient prophet Enoch, but even he was not immune from the trials and tribulations of mortality. Not the least of his trials was the challenge of overcoming great feelings of inadequacy. When called of the Lord, Enoch replied: "Why is it that I have found favour in thy sight, and am but a lad, and all the people hate me; for I am slow of speech; wherefore am I thy servant?" (Moses 6:31.) These feelings of complete inadequacy are mirrored by newly called Sunday School and Primary teachers, Relief Society presidents, bishops, and General Authorities.

Notwithstanding Enoch's weaknesses, the Lord promised him that " the mountains shall flee before you, and the rivers shall turn from their course; and thou shalt abide in me, and I in you; therefore walk with me" (Moses 6:34). And Enoch did walk with God, and as he went among the people he testified "against their works; and all men were offended because of him" (Moses 6:37–38). Nevertheless he persisted in his ministry, and notwithstanding many wars and much bloodshed Enoch led his people in righteousness, and "the Lord came and dwelt with his people. . . . And the Lord called his people ZION, because they were of one heart and one mind, and dwelt in righteousness; and there was no poor among them." (Moses 7:13–18.)

The Lord subsequently showed Enoch a panoramic view of the inhabitants of the earth throughout time, and Enoch beheld that his city of Zion, *"in the process of time, was taken up into heaven"* (Moses 7:21; emphasis added). Enoch later foresaw the time of Noah when the floods would cover the entire earth and swallow up all of the earth's wicked inhabitants, and "as Enoch saw this, he had bitterness of soul, and wept over his brethren, and said unto the heavens: I will refuse to be comforted; but the Lord said unto Enoch: Lift up your heart, and be glad; and look. . . . And behold, Enoch saw the day of the coming of the Son of Man, even in the flesh; and his soul rejoiced." (Moses 7:43–47.)

The Savior's Living Water

The coming of the Son of Man, the Savior of the world, was indeed a great cause to rejoice. His entire earthly ministry was spent in teaching, healing, comforting, and edifying others. On one occasion Jesus entered the city of Sychar in Samaria and, somewhat weary from His journey, came to Jacob's well, where He asked a Samaritan woman for a drink of water. She was somewhat surprised at His request inasmuch as "the Jews have no dealings with the Samaritans." He told her that if she knew who He was, she would have asked a drink of Him who would be able to give her living water which would be "a well of water springing up into everlasting life" (John 4:14). The living water is the gospel of Jesus Christ with all of the saving and exalting doctrines, counsel, commandments, covenants, ordinances, and promised blessings (see D&C 63:23; D&C 84:18–21; 107:18–20).

Near the end of the Old Testament, Zechariah recorded his vision of the Savior's Second Coming, when He shall stand upon the Mount of Olives and "living waters shall go out from Jerusalem: half of them toward the former [or Mediterranean] sea, and half of them toward the hinder [or Dead] sea" (Zechariah 14:8). Of this same event, Ezekiel prophesied that these living waters would become as a great river too large to pass over, and this river would "go down into the desert, and go into the sea: which being brought forth into the sea, the waters [of the Dead Sea] shall be healed. . . . And every thing shall live whither the river cometh." (Ezekiel 47:8–9.) Elsewhere we have observed that these two prophecies are profound both in their geological predictions and in their metaphorical promises (see *Your Agency: Handle with Care* [Salt Lake City: Bookcraft, 1996], p. 103).

Of all the places on earth, the Dead Sea is one of the most inhospitable to life. Even the scorching Sahara Desert sustains certain plants that are able to survive in that hot, arid climate by sinking their roots to great depths sufficient to provide them with needed moisture. Various reptiles and insects burrow into the sand and find refuge from the intense desert heat and are thus able to survive. The frigid Arctic regions of the North provide a home for polar bears and caribou, and in the southern hemisphere penguins are able to survive in the extremely cold environment of Antarctica. But the Dead Sea, because of its extreme salinity, is hostile to all living organisms with the possible exception of certain bacteria and a few halophytes (plants able to survive in extremely salty soil). But no fish or other forms of animal life are able to survive in this hostile environment; hence the origin of its name—the Dead Sea. (See "Dead Sea," *Encyclopedia Britannica*, [Chicago: Encyclopedia Britannica, Inc., 1981], 5:525.)

In prophesying of the healing influence of the living waters upon the Dead Sea, the Lord's prophets have chosen the most challenging example—the worst case scenario, if you will—and therein lies the profound promise. If the living waters can heal the Dead Sea, one of the most hostile and hopeless environments on earth, then the living waters can most assuredly irrigate and heal the parched desert of a dead marriage. The living waters can certainly revive relationships between business partners and neighbors that have fallen into estrangement. The living waters can resuscitate relationships between parents and children and between brothers and sisters, and can refresh a wilting testimony after years of inactivity in the Church. The living waters can make us clean and whole again. The living waters can wash away anguish and replenish parched deserts of discouragement, hopelessness, and despair with flowering faith and the fruits of the Spirit.

How can we drink deeply from the living waters? James testified that "the . . . fervent prayer of a righteous man availeth much" (James 5:16). This was something to which the Prophet Joseph Smith could attest, for the answer to his first vocal prayer has become a great source of comfort to millions of our Father's children throughout the earth and to unseen millions beyond the veil of mortality. Everyone needs a sacred grove where he can call down the powers of heaven "with all the energy of heart, that [we] may be filled with [the pure love of Christ]," (Moroni 7:48) for hearts full of love have no room for doubt and despair. A heart filled with love has no place for anger or anguish, revenge or retribution, envy or covetousness, for a heart filled with love is full.

There are many sources of anguish in our lives, including debilitating guilt, shame, and fear, but the anxiety of parents who have difficulty in adequately feeding their children ranks among the most poignant sources of anguish in mortality. President Thomas S. Monson described such a case—the Ballantyne family in Star Valley, Wyoming. An older son in the family related many years later that his father would often leave home to work for other farmers in the area in order to help make ends meet. On one occasion when his father was away, the family gathered for family prayers and for dinner, which, on this particular evening during the Christmas season, consisted of a glass of milk for each of the children. The young son noticed that his mother took no milk for herself, but she replied she was not hungry. He recounted the following sacred solution to their problem:

It worried me. We drank our milk and went to bed, but I could not sleep. I got up and tiptoed down the stairs, and there was Mother, in the middle of the floor, kneeling in prayer. She did not hear me as I came down in my bare feet, and I dropped to my knees and heard her say, "Heavenly Father, there is no food in our house. Please, Father, touch the heart of somebody so that my children will not be hungry in the morning."

When she finished her prayer, she looked around and saw that I had heard; and she said to me, somewhat embarrassed, "Now, you run along, son. Everything will be all right."

I went to bed, assured by Mother's faith. The next morning, I was awakened by the sounds of pots and pans in the kitchen and the aroma of cooking food. I went down to the kitchen, and I said, "Mother, I thought you said there was no food."

All she said to me was, "Well, my boy, didn't you think the Lord would answer my prayer?" I received no further explanation than that.

Years passed, and I went away to college. I got married, and I returned to see the old folks. Bishop Gardner, now reaching up to a ripe age, said to me, "My son, let me tell you of a Christmas experience that I had with your family. I had finished my chores, and we had had supper. I was sitting by the fireplace reading the newspaper. Suddenly, I heard a voice that said, 'Sister Ballantyne doesn't have any food in her house.' I thought it was my wife speaking and said, 'What did you say, Mother?' She came in wiping her hands on her apron and said, 'Did you call me, Father?'

" 'No, I didn't say anything to you, but I heard a voice which spoke to me.'

" 'What did it say?' she asked.

" 'It said that Sister Ballantyne didn't have any food in her house.'

" 'Well, then,' said Mother, 'you had better put on your shoes and your coat and take some food to Sister Ballantyne.' In the dark of that winter's night, I harnessed the team and placed in the wagon bed a sack of flour, a quarter section of beef, some bottled fruit, and loaves of newly baked bread. The weather was cold, but a warm glow filled my soul as your mother welcomed me and I presented her with the food. God had heard a mother's prayer." (Thomas S. Monson, "Christmas Gifts, Christmas Blessings," Ensign, December 1995, p. 5.)

The prayer of the righteous availeth much. Indeed, fervent prayer unlocks the floodgates of the living water, which washes away the cumulative debris in our lives and refreshes our

parched and selfish sin-sick souls. Spiritual roots are strengthened, and as the living water reaches withered leaves they are
renewed and lend strength and shade to budding testimonies
which blossom and flourish.

Drinking deeply from the scriptures helps us lay claim to the
Lord's promise that "with joy shall ye draw water out of the
wells of salvation" (2 Nephi 22:3). Fasting makes sponges of our
souls so that we might absorb the living water in greater measure. Participating in the ordinances of the gospel and keeping
our covenants help clear the channels through which the living
waters flow. Just as the Dead Sea will be healed, the salt in our
tears will be removed as the God of comfort wipes away all the
tears from all the faces regardless of the source of those tears
(see Isaiah 25:8).

We Will Receive Comfort

In January 1994 I was assigned to attend the Pocatello
Idaho Stake conference, where I enjoyed meeting several Saints
with whom I had attended Pocatello High School some years
previously. It was also a pleasure to meet many new friends,
among whom were Joyce and Jeff Underwood. Prior to the Sat-
urday evening meeting I asked Joyce if she would share her testimony with the Saints. As she began her remarks, all eyes and
hearts were riveted upon her as she recounted the events of the
family tragedy that had happened to them the previous summer.

On a mid-summer evening their young daughter Jeralee had
gone throughout the neighbourhood collecting money for her
paper route. When the late summer sun began to set and Jeralee
had not returned home her parents became very concerned,
and as darkness began to fall their apprehension increased to
the point where they eventually called the police, who sent out
an all-points bulletin describing little Jeralee's clothing and her
last known whereabouts. The first night was an absolute nightmare filled with anxiety and anguish.

Several hundred neighbors and other concerned citizens of Pocatello joined in an extensive search for the missing girl. Joyce told the congregation, "As the days dragged on we prayed so hard, and Jeff and I became so close to each other, and we became so close to the Lord, we almost hated for the week to end." But eventually one of the detectives working on the case came to their home to inform them that Jeralee's mortal remains had been located and the police had a confessed murderer in their custody. A press conference was held in which some of the details of the brutal murder were described by the police, and then the reporters turned to the Underwoods for their response. In an emotion-filled voice, Joyce said: "I have learned a lot about love this week, and I also know there is a lot of hate. I have looked at the love and want to feel that love, and not the hate. We can forgive."

Elder James E. Faust and Elder Joe J. Christensen represented the Brethren at Jeralee's funeral (see James E. Faust, "Five Loaves and Two Fishes," Ensign, May 1994, p. 6). The spirit of the occasion was understandably very subdued, but absent from that memorial service were feelings of vengeance and hatred as an Apostle of the Lord blessed that sorrowing family by the apostolic power of the priesthood he held. The grieving parents had claimed and received the Savior's promise: "I will not leave you comfortless: I will come to you" (John 14:18). That promise is not reserved just for the Underwoods but is given to any and all who will come to the God of all comfort with forgiving hearts and accept the invitation eloquently expressed in that hopeful hymn "Come, Ye Disconsolate":

Come, Ye Disconsolate

Come, ye disconsolate, where'er ye languish;
Come to the mercy seat, fervently kneel.
Here bring your wounded hearts;
Here tell your anguish.
Earth has no sorrow that heaven cannot heal.

Joy of the desolate, light of the straying,
Hope of the penitent, fadeless and pure!
Here speaks the Comforter, tenderly saying,
"Earth has no sorrow that heaven cannot cure."

Here see the Bread of Life; see waters flowing
Forth from the throne of God, pure from above.
Come to the feast of love; come, ever knowing
Earth has no sorrow but heaven can remove.
(Thomas Moore, *Hymns*, no. 115)

Two

Comfort Those in Need of Comfort

As THE SAVIOR'S EARTHLY MINISTRY BEGAN to draw to a close He prepared His disciples for His eventual departure, explaining: "In my Father's house are many mansions: if it were not so, I would have told you. I go to prepare a place for you" (John 14:2). He then assured them: ". . . I will pray the Father, and he shall give you another Comforter, that he may abide with you for ever" (John 14:16).

The power and influence of the Holy Ghost are explained throughout the scriptures. The Comforter will "teach [us] all things, and bring all things to [our] remembrance" (John 14:26). He will also testify of the Savior (see John 15:26) and of the Father (see 3 Nephi 11:32–36), and He will guide us "into all truth" and show us "things to come" (John 16:13; see also Alma 30:46). As a member of the Godhead He will comfort us in our hour of need (see 1 Nephi 21:13; Alma 17:10; 3 Nephi 12:4; D&C 100:15; 101:14) and quicken "all things" (D&C 33:16). (See also: Dennis E. Simmons, "His Peace," *Ensign*, May 1997, pp. 31–32.)

Those who refuse to be comforted resist the influence of a member of the Godhead in their lives, even the Holy Ghost,

the Comforter. A recurrent message throughout the Book of
Mormon is the reassurance that the Holy Spirit *strives* with us
to resist evil (see 2 Nephi 26:11; Mormon 5:16), and *entices* us
to do that which is right (see Mosiah 3:19). The Spirit *persuades*
us to do good to others (see Ether 4:11). In short, the Comforter can and will exert a very strong and active influence in
our lives if we will but permit Him to do so. When we refuse to
be comforted we become susceptible to Satan's shabby substi-
tutes whereby he replaces faith with doubt, hope with despair,
meekness with vengeance, and he supplants long-suffering and
compassion with strident demands for immediate retribution.

Forgiveness in Lieu of Retribution

In the early days of the restored Church the principle was
established that "the commission of crime should be punished
according to the nature of the offense . . . and for the public
peace and tranquility all men should step forward and use their
ability in bringing offenders against good laws to punishment"
(D&C 134:8). Occasionally the intent of the heart of a well-
meaning priesthood leader is misunderstood as he counsels a
victim of injustice or abuse to follow the Savior's admonition to
forgive the perpetrator of the evil deed. Sometimes that counsel
is misconstrued to indicate that the priesthood leader is soft on
sin and winks at criminal behavior and that he is seeking to
cover up the egregious sins of the perpetrator while ignoring the
victim's needs for justice and comfort. Generally, the perpetrators will be dealt with in the courts of the land, and in Church
disciplinary councils in the Lord's own way.

The Lord has revealed that those who fail to repent should
be brought "before the church" for disciplinary action, "not because ye forgive not, having not compassion, but that ye may be
justified in the eyes of the law, that ye may not offend him who
is your lawgiver." (D&C 64:12–13; see also D&C 42:37; Mosiah
26:36; Alma 1:24; 3 Nephi 18:31.) The outcome of a Church

disciplinary council is maintained in confidence, so most people will never know of the severity of the discipline, nor will they know of the anguish of errant men and women who have eventually been brought to a "bright recollection" of their guilt (see 2 Nephi 9:14; Mosiah 2:38 and Alma 11:43). The Lord admonished those who have been severely wronged to say in their hearts, "let God judge between me and thee, and reward thee according to thy deeds" (D&C 64:11). The Savior died not only for our sins, but also for the sins of those who have offended us; thus, as our Advocate with the Father, it is for Him to decide who shall be forgiven. We are charged to forgive our debtors as we would be forgiven of our own debts.

The voice of the Lord instructed Alma that if a sinner "confess his sins before thee and me, and repenteth in the sincerity of his heart, him shall ye forgive, and I will forgive him also. Yea, and as often as my people repent will I forgive them their trespasses against me. And ye shall also forgive one another your trespasses; for verily I say unto you, he that forgiveth not his neighbor's trespasses when he says that he repents, the same hath brought himself under condemnation." (Mosiah 26:29–31.) This divine counsel to forgive our neighbors and to let God be the judge provides great comfort to those who let go of feelings of hurt, hate and vengeance as they pray to be forgiven of their debts as they forgive their debtors. As we forgive others, the Comforter will, indeed, comfort us and provide us with peace beyond our fondest expectations.

A few days after speaking at a stake conference session about the Atonement and the need to forgive others, I received a letter from a distressed family who had attended the meeting. Their letter implied that there are simply times when it is impossible to forgive others who offend us. They then explained their particular case in point. It seems that they hired a local building contractor, a good member of the Church, to build them a new house. The contractor gave them a firm bid with a guaranteed price. At the completion of the project they moved into the new house only to discover that their dream home was a nightmare. The roof leaked whenever it rained, some of the plumbing fixtures leaked, some of the lights did not function properly, and some of the floors squeaked.

This good Latter-day Saint family felt they had been "taken for a ride" by their friendly neighborhood contractor. They had bitterly complained to the contractor about the poor quality of his work and they demanded that he make things right. He explained to them that between the time he quoted them a guaranteed price for the home and the day he declared the project finished there had been numerous price increases in materials. Just before the foundation was poured there had been a large increase in the cost of cement. There were also concomitant cost increases in lumber, sheet rock, and in plumbing and electrical supplies. Then, to make matters even worse for him, labor costs increased unexpectedly. The contractor, though he had the best of intentions at the outset, was required to instruct all of the subcontractors to do their work as fast as possible, because he was strapped for finances. The bottom line was that the contractor had actually lost money on this project and a few other projects and simply had no money to correct all the problems that needed to be rectified.

The family who wrote me the letter requested that Church leaders apply pressure to this hapless contractor to cajole him into correcting the building deficiencies in their home. After investigating the matter with local Church leaders, we called the family and urged them to forgive their contractor who, in the judgment of his local leaders, had done the very best he could under the circumstances. If the family were not willing to provide him with additional funds to cover his cost overruns, then he simply was not financially able to correct the roofing and plumbing and electrical problems. But the family remained adamant: "A deal is a deal," they said. "He promised to build us a house for a certain price and he reneged on his promise."

I sent this family a copy of Elder Boyd K. Packer's general

conference address, "Balm of Gilead," in which he declared: "We see so much unnecessary suffering, so many who cripple themselves spiritually carrying burdens which could be put down. Many suffer from real misfortune and injustice. Sadly, some only imagine that they do. In either case, self-inflicted penalties soon become cruel and unusual punishment."

He continued: "Some frustrations we must endure without really solving the problem. Some things that ought to be put in order are not put in order because we cannot control them. Things we cannot solve, we must survive."

Elder Packer concluded: "If you resent someone for something he has done—or failed to do—forget it. . . . If you brood constantly over a loss or a past mistake, look ahead—settle it.

"We call that forgiveness. Forgiveness is powerful spiritual medicine. To extend forgiveness, that soothing balm, to those who have offended you is to heal. And, more difficult yet, when the need is there, forgive yourself!" (Boyd K. Packer, "Balm of Gilead," *Ensign*, November 1987, pp. 16–18.)

Several weeks passed and I hoped and prayed that President Packer's comforting counsel would find lodging in their hearts. Then one day I received a telephone call from the young wife and mother of the distressed family. Because their new home represented so many unpleasant memories, they had decided to sell it. She assured me that they had candidly informed the new buyers of all the problems with the house, and the buyers were willing to invest the additional funds to make all the necessary repairs. Another home had been located and the formerly distressed family was now happily preparing to move into an affordable home which was in good condition.

Before concluding our phone conversation, this lovely sister then explained the real reason for her call. She said words to this effect: "The other day, I realized it wasn't just enough to sell one house and move to another. We needed to forgive the contractor who had caused us so much distress. I began to realize he had probably done the best he could under the circumstances,

so we baked his family a cake, and we personally delivered it to
the contractor's home. When he came to the door we told him
we had forgiven him and hoped he could forgive us as well. You
should have seen the relieved look on his face, and you can't
believe what a good feeling that gave us, now that it's over!"

In Ulster, Northern Ireland, there has been a pattern of repeated retribution in the continuing conflict between the
Catholic Irish Republican Army, who seek independence from
the United Kingdom, and the Protestant loyalists or unionists
who wish to remain subjects of the British monarchy. Every
death of a Catholic is seemingly avenged by the death of a
Protestant, and when a Protestant is killed the life of a Catholic
is often taken. Amid the sectarian violence and the hatred
there arises the occasional voice of those who take the teachings of the Savior seriously and who have learned to forgive,
even when it is most difficult. One such person is a devout
Catholic, Laurence Martin of Craigavon, North Ireland. In July
of 1997 his beautiful eighteen-year-old daughter Bernadette was
"shot four times in the head at close range as she lay asleep at
the house of her Protestant boyfriend in the staunchly loyalist
village of Aghalee" (Nicholas Watt, "Let Her Be the Last Victim, Says Ulster Father," *The Times*, London, July 17, 1997, p.
2). Notwithstanding the great heart-ache that Laurence Martin
and his wife Margaret feel, Mr. Martin issued a plea for other
Catholics to refrain from any acts of vengeance. Said he: "We
do not want any repercussions or people claiming reprisals. If
her death is the last death in this country, then maybe it is
worth something and we can live in peace.

"She was such a special girl; we loved her so very much. It is
hard to believe she really is gone. Whoever did that, I have no
feelings for them. I can forgive them." (Ibid.)

Rita Restorick is another forgiving citizen of Northern Ireland. Her son, Stephen, was gunned down by an Irish Republican Army sniper and was buried on his twenty-fourth birthday.
Mrs. Restorick said: "I want peace in Northern Ireland so no

other mother has to go through what I have gone through, and what so many other mothers have gone through in the past 28 years" (Martin Fletcher, "Bereaved Mother Leads Peace Vigil," ibid., September 16, 1997, p. 2). She was joined in a peace vigil by a dozen other women, both Protestants and Catholics, who had also lost loved ones in the ongoing senseless sectarian violence. One of these compatriots was Thelma Campbell, whose eighteen-year-old brother was riddled with seventeen bullets while on military patrol in 1972. Mrs. Campbell said: "There's no other way to go forward except by forgiving each other." (Ibid.)

Jesus' Example Is a Source of Comfort

Elder Neal A. Maxwell posed a series of introspective questions for times when we begin to feel that the Savior may have abandoned us in our hour of need, an hour in which we perhaps refuse to be comforted. Elder Maxwell asks:

— Can we, even in the depth of disease, tell Him anything at all about suffering?

— Can those who yearn for hearth or home instruct Him as to what it is like to be homeless or on the move?

— Can we really counsel Him about being misrepresented, misunderstood, or betrayed?

— Can we educate Him regarding injustice or compare failures of judicial systems with the Giver of the Law, who, in divine dignity, endured its substantive and procedural perversion?

— And when we feel so alone, can we presume to teach Him who trod "the wine press alone" anything at all about feeling forsaken?

— Cannot the childless who crave children count on His empathy? For He loved children and said, "Of such is the kingdom of heaven."

— Do we presume to instruct Him in either compassion or
mercy?
— Can we excuse our compromises because of the powerful
temptations of status seeking?
— Can we lecture Him on liberty, He who set us free from
our last enemies—sin and death?
— Can those concerned with nourishing the poor advise
Him concerning feeding the multitudes?
— Can those who are concerned with medicine instruct
Him about healing the sick?
— Or can we inform the Atoner about feeling the sting of
ingratitude when one's service goes unappreciated or un-
noticed?
— Should we seek to counsel Him in courage? Should we
rush forth eagerly to show Him our mortal medals—our
scratches and bruises—He who bears His five special
wounds? (Neal A. Maxwell, "O, Divine Redeemer," *Ensign*, November 1981, pp. 8–10.)

Paul Comforts Others

The Apostle Paul admonished the Corinthians to comfort
others in tribulation by the comfort they themselves had received from "the God of all comfort." (2 Corinthians 1:3–4.)
Paul practiced the gospel he preached, for there were many
times in his life when he received comfort from on high and
graciously extended that comfort to others. On his third missionary journey he travelled to Macedonia, Thessalonica,
Athens, Corinth, and Ephesus, and though he had been warned
that evil men lay in wait for him if he returned to Jerusalem,
Paul nevertheless returned and was, indeed, arrested. (See Acts
20–21.) He was brought before the high priest, Ananias, who
ordered that he be smitten on the mouth. The chief captain of
the guard, fearing that Paul would be "pulled in pieces" by his

accusers, took him to the castle to spend the night in protective custody. That night "the Lord stood by him, and said, Be of good cheer, Paul: for as thou hast testified of me in Jerusalem, so must thou bear witness also at Rome." (See Acts 23:1–11.) The God of comfort had not left him comfortless.

Paul was subsequently brought before Felix, the Governor of Judea, who judged him and afterward told him: "Go thy way for this time; when I have a convenient season, I will call for thee" (Acts 24:25). Two years later Felix was succeeded by Festus, who allowed Paul to plead his case before King Agrippa. After Agrippa had heard the moving testimony of Paul's conversion, he said to Paul, "Almost thou persuadest me to be a Christian" (Acts 26:28). Although Agrippa and Festus acknowledged among themselves that Paul had done nothing "worthy of death and bonds," they ordered him sent to Rome because, as a Roman citizen, he had appealed to Caesar's judgment in the case (see Acts 26:31–32). This, of course, was the Lord's means of bringing one of His Apostles to the heart of the Roman Empire.

Before embarking for Rome, Paul issued a prophetic warning of tempestuous seas ahead, but the masters of the ship ignored his warnings and they set sail against all hazards. True to Paul's warning, the seas became extremely perilous and Paul, who had been comforted of the Lord, now became an instrument in providing comfort to those who were terrorized by the stormy sea. Paul boldly exhorted the sailors to "be of good cheer," promising them that "there shall be no loss of any man's life among you, but of the ship. For there stood by me this night the angel of God, whose I am, and whom I serve, saying, Fear not, Paul; thou must be brought before Caesar: and, lo, God hath given thee all them that sail with thee. Wherefore, sirs, be of good cheer: for I believe God, that it shall be even as it was told me" (Acts 27:22–25). As prophesied, the ship was wrecked but those aboard "escaped all safe to land" (Acts 27:44).

Joseph Smith Comforts the Saints

The Prophet Joseph Smith had some experiences with imprisonment not unlike those experienced by Paul. After languishing in Liberty Jail for several months under extremely harsh conditions, and amid countless rumors that the Saints were being subjected to all manner of persecution, in a moment of dire anguish in March of 1839 the Prophet implored the Lord: "O God, where art thou? And where is the pavilion that covereth thy hiding place?" (D&C 121:1.) And the God of comfort responded: "My son, peace be unto thy soul; thine adversity and thine afflictions shall be but a small moment; and then, if thou endure it well, God shall exalt thee on high; thou shalt triumph over all thy foes" (D&C 121:7–8). The Lord assured him "that all these things shall give thee experience, and shall be for thy good" (D&C 122:7). It is significant that later in the Prophet Joseph's lengthy epistle to the Saints, written while he was still in Liberty Jail, he exhorted the Saints to "cheerfully do all things that lie in our power; and then may we stand still, with the utmost assurance, to see the salvation of God, and for his arm to be revealed" (D&C 123:17). Like Paul, Joseph had received comfort from the God of all comfort and had graciously extended that same comfort to "them which are in any trouble, by the comfort wherewith [he himself had been] comforted of God" (2 Corinthians 1:3–4).

An interesting sequel to the Prophet's imprisonment and eventual freedom was W. W. Phelps's request for readmission to full fellowship among the Saints. On 4 September 1837 the Prophet had received a revelation that "John Whitmer and William W. Phelps have done those things which are not pleasing in my sight, therefore if they repent not they shall be removed out of their places" (*History of the Church* 2:511—hereafter cited as *HC*). Five months later, on 5 February 1838, a disciplinary council was convened to consider the actions of David Whitmer, John Whitmer, and Brother Phelps. The council voted to censure these brethren, and on 10 February at a meeting of the high council Brother Phelps was informed that he could no longer serve as a clerk in signing and recording licenses. In a high council meeting held on 10 March 1838 the council preferred charges of persistent unchristian-like conduct against W. W. Phelps and John Whitmer, and they were formally excommunicated. (See *HC* 3:6–8.)

In early August of 1838 W. W. Phelps resigned his position as postmaster at Far West, thus distancing himself further from the Saints against a background of increasing hostility and mob violence against the Saints by Missouri residents. On 27 October that year Governor Lilburn W. Boggs issued his infamous exterminating order: "The Mormons must be treated as enemies and must be exterminated or driven from the state" (*HC* 3:175). This order further fomented the mob violence, which led to the massacre at Haun's Mill on October 30 (see *HC* 3:183–186). On 1 November the Prophet Joseph and other Church leaders, who had been recently betrayed to the mob militia, were ordered to be summarily shot in the public square at Far West. It was only through the courageous intervention of Brigadier-General A.W. Doniphan, who refused to obey the order, that the lives of the Prophet and his brethren were spared. (See *HC* 3:190–91.)

The captives were then taken under armed guard to Richmond, and it was in the Richmond jail that the Prophet rebuked the guards after he and his companions had been made to listen to their "obscene jests, the horrid oaths, the dreadful blasphemies and filthy language" (*HC* 3:208). At the end of November the Prophet and several other brethren were transferred to the cold, dank jail in Liberty, Missouri, where they languished for the next four and a half months, until on 6 April 1839 Judge Austin A. King ordered their removal under guard to Daviess County for another trial beginning 9 April. After procuring a change of venue to Boone County, on the evening of 15 April the Prophet and his fellow prisoners took leave of their intoxicated guard and departed for home.

On 29 June 1840, more than two years after his excommunication from the Church, William W. Phelps wrote from Dayton, Ohio, to the Prophet requesting readmission into the Church: ". . . I am as the prodigal son, though I never doubt or disbelieve the fulness of the Gospel. . . . I have seen the folly of my way, and I tremble at the gulf I have passed. . . . I know my situation, you know it, and God knows it, and I want to be saved if my friends will help me. . . ." (HC 4:141–42.) A response to his letter was mailed on 22 July 1840 by the Prophet, who said, among many other things:

> Inasmuch as long-suffering, patience, and mercy have ever characterized the dealings of our heavenly Father towards the humble and penitent, I feel disposed to copy the example, cherish the same principles, and by so doing be a savior of my fellow men.
>
> It is true, that we have suffered much in consequence of your behavior—the cup of gall, already full enough for mortals to drink, was indeed filled to overflowing when you turned against us. . . . However, the cup has been drunk, the will of our Father has been done, and we are yet alive, for which we thank the Lord. . . . Believing your confession to be real, and your repentance genuine, I shall be happy once again to give you the right hand of fellowship, and rejoice over the returning prodigal. . . .
>
> "Come on, dear brother, since the war is past,
> For friends at first, are friends again at last." (HC 4:162–64.)

In his letter the Prophet Joseph very appropriately reproved Brother Phelps for his past transgressions, which had contributed to the further persecution of the Saints, but it was fitting that the Saints voted to accept him back into full fellowship in the kingdom and that the Prophet extended to him the comforting hand of friendship and fellowship.

Alma Comforts Amulek

As the high priest over the Nephite Church, Alma "began to deliver the word of God unto the people" (Alma 5:1). Eventually he came to the city of Ammonihah, whose residents cast him out. The same angel who initially had come to him in his wayward youth appeared again to him on this mission and commanded him to return to Ammonihah. (See Alma 8:9–18; Mosiah 27:13–15.) It was there that he encountered Amulek, who had been prepared by an angel to meet Alma. After staying with Amulek for several days Alma was inspired to call him to serve as his missionary companion, and Amulek became a very effective teacher of the gospel, being "filled with the Holy Ghost" (see Alma 8:19–30).

In the course of their missionary labors in Ammonihah Alma and Amulek were arrested and taken before the chief judge of the land. After being bound they were forced to witness the martyrdom of the believers, who were cast into a fire and consumed. This holocaust was so painful and traumatic to Amulek that he pleaded with Alma to exercise their priesthood power to save these faithful people from such a horrible death, but Alma replied: "The Spirit constraineth me that I must not stretch forth mine hand; for behold the Lord receiveth them up unto himself, in glory; and he doth suffer that . . . the people may do this thing unto them, according to the hardness of their hearts, that the judgments which he shall exercise upon them in his wrath may be just; and the blood of the innocent shall stand as a witness against them, yea, and cry mightily against them at the last day" (Alma 14:11).

Before his mission Alma had experienced extreme anguish over his own personal sins, even being "tormented with the pains of hell," but as he repented he had been comforted of the Lord (see Alma 36). Now Amulek had experienced not only rejection by his friends and kindred (see Alma 15:16) but also the anguish of witnessing faithful Saints being martyred for their beliefs. Thus he felt bereft of comfort, so Alma took Amulek "to his own house, and did administer unto him in his tribulations, and strengthened him in the Lord" (Alma 15:18). It is well for mission presidents and stake presidents to remember that sometimes not only the sheep but also the shepherds need to be strengthened.

Comfort After Being Called

In the midst of a sudden family tragedy, the need for comfort from others is self-evident. We are sometimes less sensitive, however, to the need for comfort in the wake of receiving a Church calling, which is a great honor but also a formidable responsibility. Many a newly called bishop or Relief Society president is absolutely overwhelmed with feelings of unworthiness and inadequacy, and at times such as these a comforting word of assurance from friends and loved ones is very much in order. President Spencer W. Kimball disclosed that he wept in the arms of his beloved Camilla after receiving his calling to the holy apostleship.

Such experiences are by no means unusual. I recall a sacrament meeting in which a young father in our ward, with tears streaming down his cheeks, expressed his fears and overwhelming feelings of unworthiness after having been called to serve as a mission president. After the meeting the members came forward with words of comfort, encouragement, and good cheer; and the Lord was able to perform many miracles through this humble servant, who served with distinction and whose service really made a difference in the kingdom.

After Mary had been told by the angel Gabriel that she had "found favour with God," one can only imagine the overwhelming feelings of her heart when he informed her, "thou shalt conceive in thy womb, and bring forth a son, and shalt call his name JESUS." (Luke 1:30–31.) We can imagine that she was astonished by the weight of that responsibility, and her initial inclination was to seek out her older cousin Elisabeth, whom the angel said was also expecting a man child "in her old age." So Mary "went into the hill country with haste, into a city of Juda" to the home of Elisabeth and Zacharias, and when Elisabeth saw her cousin she said in a loud voice: "Blessed art thou among women, and blessed is the fruit of thy womb. And whence is this to me, that the mother of my Lord should come to me?" (Luke 1:36–43.) That Elisabeth also knew her secret was of great comfort to Mary, as she meekly exclaimed: "My soul doth magnify the Lord, and my spirit hath rejoiced in God" (Luke 1:46–47).

One of the great burdens of many callings in the kingdom is the necessity of keeping certain information confidential, so it was comforting to both Mary and Elisabeth to know that each of them had independently been informed by an angel that they had been given special assignments by Deity to prepare young sons for sacred future missions. Elisabeth's son would preach repentance and "make ready a people prepared for the Lord" (Luke 1:17), and he would baptize by water. Mary's Son would baptize by fire and would take upon Him the sins of the world and eventually die that all mankind should live. A little more than thirty-three years later, when that final moment arrived on Golgotha, the Savior, ever attentive to the needs of His mother until His dying breath, charged the Apostle John to comfort His mother, "and from that hour that disciple took her unto his own home" (John 19:27). Jesus had promised His disciples that He would not leave them comfortless, and that promise was even more assuring to His mother.

Comfort from Cousins

Mary and Elisabeth were not the only cousins to become mutual sources of comfort. Brad Taggart was an art student at Utah State University in search of a model for a sculpturing project. At the suggestion of his instructor, Brad visited a retirement home to see if one of the elderly residents would be amenable to serving as his model. Upon reviewing the list of residents, it became readily apparent that an excellent candidate would be the former President of Utah State University,

Glen Taggart, who happened to be a cousin to Brad's grand-father. President Taggart had recently suffered a stroke and was also waging a battle against cancer and was rather frail, so he asked Brad to sculpt a bust of him as he would have looked during his presidency of USU. With the aid of photos taken during the years 1968 to 1979, Brad was able to capture Glen's countenance of two decades previously. The project was funded by Glen's brother, Spencer L. Taggart, who opted to attend all of the sculpting sessions.

> "Actually, it was therapy for myself, Glen and Spence. It helped Spence regain his brother and helped me get to know another part of my family," Brad said. . . .
>
> Brad remembers one day, in particular, when Glen seemed to be extra focused on the project. Trying to catch just the right angle of facial features, Brad asked him to turn his head away from the sculpture. But Glen gently resisted and tried to explain something about the piece.
>
> When Brad could not understand, Glen rose from his wheelchair, walked over to the sculpture and pointed to a small section needing to be adjusted. This part had escaped Brad's artistic eye momentarily, but Glen had noticed every detail. "It was like he was doing the work himself, by proxy," Brad fondly recalls.
>
> Brad says he feels personal involvement with the sculpture helped remind Glen of the great man he was and still is. Despite the setbacks caused by the stroke, Glen found within himself a new beginning. "I believe it changed his whole life," Brad stated.
>
> Commenting on his brother's change, Spencer wrote in a personal poem, "Glen began the working sessions in a wheel chair [and] ended them walking with a cane. . . .
>
> "This project has brought back something of Glen's former self—renewed hope and self-worth." (Kerry Griffin, "Sculpting Lives," *The Herald Journal*, Logan, Utah, April 5, 1994, p. 11.)

When grandchildren tape record interviews and conversations with aging grandparents, a similar kind of comforting miracle occurs. Aging grandparents, whose major focus may have been upon their increasing aches and pains, experience a refreshing return in time to a day when they were young and vigorous and their days were filled with significant accomplishments. Reciprocal expressions of affection do much to comfort members of both the older and the younger generation, and teachable teen-agers just might gain a pearl or two of wisdom that will serve them well as a source of comfort in the years to come.

Comfort from Modern Prophets

Modern-day prophets are instruments of the Lord in providing comfort to his Saints. President Harold B. Lee observed that the gospel "comforts the afflicted and afflicts the comfortable." One who was no stranger to some of the vicious vicissitudes of life was President Spencer W. Kimball. His life was marked with countless afflictions of the flesh, including bouts with severe boils, Bell's palsy, throat cancer, and coronary heart disease requiring open heart surgery on more than one occasion. Precisely because he had undergone the Refiner's fire and had received comfort from the God of all comfort, he was in an empathetic position to be able to comfort those in need of comfort.

To those bereaved by the loss of a loved one, President Kimball sensitively explained: "If we looked at mortality as the whole of existence, then pain, sorrow, failure, and short life would be calamity. But if we look upon life as an eternal thing stretching far into the premortal past and on into the eternal post-death future, then all happenings may be put in proper perspective." (Spencer W. Kimball, *Faith Precedes the Miracle* [Salt Lake City: Deseret Book Co., 1972], p. 97.)

Viewing suffering and loss within the context of the Great Plan of Happiness, President Kimball continued his comforting counsel: "If all the sick for whom we pray were healed, if all the righteous were protected and the wicked destroyed, the whole program of the Father would be annulled and the basic principle of the gospel, free agency, would be ended. No man would have to live by faith." (Ibid.)

Elder Orson F. Whitney eloquently observed that "no pain that we suffer, no trial that we experience is wasted. It ministers to our education, to the development of such qualities as patience, faith, fortitude and humility. All that we suffer and all that we endure, especially when we endure it patiently, builds up our characters, purifies our hearts, expands our souls, and makes us more tender and charitable, more worthy to be called the children of God." (Cited in *Faith Precedes the Miracle*, p. 98.)

President Kimball assured those discomfited by a death following a priesthood administration that

> the sick will be healed if the ordinance is performed, if there is sufficient faith, and if the ill one is "not appointed unto death" [see D&C 42:44–48]. But there are three factors, all of which should be satisfied. Many do not comply with the ordinances, and great numbers are unwilling or incapable of exercising sufficient faith. But the other factor also looms important: If they are not appointed unto death.
>
> Everyone must die. Death is an important part of life. Of course, we are never quite ready for the change. Not knowing when it should come, we properly fight to retain our life. Yet we ought not to be afraid of death. . . .
>
> We knew before we were born that we were coming to the earth for bodies and experience and that we would have joys and sorrows, ease and pain, comforts and hardship, health and sickness, successes and disappointments, and we knew also that after a period of life we would die. We accepted all these eventualities with a glad heart, eager to accept both the favorable and unfavorable. We eagerly accepted the chance to come earthward even though it might be for only a day or a year. . . .
>
> In the face of apparent tragedy we must put our trust in God, knowing that despite our limited view his purposes will not fail. With all its troubles life offers us the tremendous privilege to grow in knowledge and wisdom, faith and works, preparing to return and share God's glory. (Ibid., pp. 103, 106.)

Like President Kimball, President Howard W. Hunter suffered more than his fair share of thorns in the flesh, especially during the last decade of his life. In 1983 he had experienced the loss of his first wife, his beloved Claire after fifty-two years of marriage. He subsequently encountered several major health challenges and major successive surgeries that left him in extreme pain and without the full use of his legs. Five years after marrying his new wife, Inis, in 1990, President Hunter was sustained as the fourteenth President of the Church. Though personally suffering severe pain and discomfort from the ravages of cancer, in his first general conference address as the newly sustained prophet President Hunter extended the following comforting invitation:

> First, I invite all members of the Church to live with ever more attention to the life and example of the Lord Jesus Christ, especially the love and hope and compassion he displayed. I pray that we will treat each other with more kindness, more patience, more courtesy and forgiveness.
>
> To those who have transgressed or been offended, we say, come back. The path of repentance, though hard at times, lifts one ever upward and leads to a perfect forgiveness."
>
> To those who are hurt or are struggling and afraid, we say, let us stand with you and dry your tears. Come back. Stand with us in The Church of Jesus Christ of Latter-day Saints. Take literally his invitation to "come follow me" (see Matthew 16:24; 19:21; Mark 8:34; 10:21; Luke 9:23; 18:22; John 21:22; D&C 38:22). He is the only sure way; he is the light of the world. (Howard W. Hunter, "Exceeding Great and Precious Promises," Ensign, November 1994, p. 8.)

President Gordon B. Hinckley is also sensitive to the pain and suffering of others. When young Gordon was but eight years of age his older brother, Stanford, died in France during World War I. When President Hinckley was but a young man of twenty his mother passed away. (See Sheri L. Dew, Go Forward with Faith: The Biography of Gordon B. Hinckley [Salt Lake City: Deseret Book Co., 1996], pp. 39, 51–52.) Through his mother's death he learned firsthand "to know something of death—the absolute devastation of children losing their mother—but also of peace without pain and the certainty that death cannot be the end of the soul" (Gordon B. Hinckley, "Some Lessons I Learned as a Boy," *Ensign*, May, 1993, p. 54).

He also knows the loneliness of leadership, having carried the great burden of serving for many years as a counselor in the First Presidency when one or more of his Brethren suffered from the infirmities and limitations incident to age. To the adult members of the Church who are unmarried, he provided the following comforting counsel:

> Sometimes you pray to the Lord with great earnestness for help, for companionship, for relief from your struggles. You wonder why your prayers are not answered as you would like them to be.
>
> We have all had that experience. But we come to know as the years pass that our Father in Heaven does hear our prayers. His wisdom is greater than ours, and we come to know that He answers our prayers even though the answers at times are difficult to discern.
>
> My heart reaches out in love to each of you. I think that in some measure, at least, I know something of your problems and your desires." (Gordon B. Hinckley, "A Conversation with Single Adults," *Ensign*, March 1997, p. 58.)

Continuing his message of hope and comfort, President Hinckley said:

> To you single women and men who wish to be married I say this, *Do not give up hope. And do not give up trying. But do give up being obsessed with it.* The chances are that if you forget about it and become anxiously engaged in other activities, the prospects will brighten immeasurably . . .
>
> I believe that for most of us the best medicine for loneliness is work and service in behalf of others. I do not minimize your problems, but I do not hesitate to say that there are many others whose problems are more serious than yours. Reach out to serve them, to help them, to encourage them. . . .
>
> Lose yourselves in the service of others. . . .
>
> To you single mothers and fathers, may I say a special word of appreciation for you. Your burdens are heavy. We know this. . . . Do the very best you can and plead with the Lord for His help that your children may grow in grace and understanding and achievement, and most importantly, in faith. If you do so, the day will come when you will get

on your knees and, with tears in your eyes, thank the Lord for His blessings upon you.

To you older women and men who are widows and widowers, how precious you are. . . .

. . . Brothers and sisters, look above your trials. Try to forget your own pain as you work to alleviate the pain of others. . . . Cultivate friends. Begin by being a good friend to others.

Share your burdens with the Lord. He has said to each of us: "Come unto me, all ye that labour and are heavy laden, and I will give you rest" (Matthew 11:28). . . .

. . . Please be assured of our love. Please be assured of our respect, of our confidence in you. Insofar as I have the right to do so, I bless you that if you will walk in faith and righteousness you will know much of happiness, you will have the temporal blessings you need, you will have friends with whom you can share your thoughts and your feelings, and you will experience the love of the Redeemer of the world. (Ibid., pp. 60–63.)

THREE

Places of Refuge

THE LORD COMMANDED MOSES TO DESIGNATE in ancient Israel six different cities to be places of refuge. These cities were set aside for the specific purpose of providing a safe haven for anyone who accidentally killed another person "unawares," or unintentionally "without enmity" (Numbers 35:6–15, 25; Deuteronomy 19:4). The Lord gave the example of two men who go into the woods to chop down some trees. One of the men has the misfortune of having the iron head of his axe fly off the handle while he is chopping wood. His neighbor has the even greater misfortune of being struck in the head by the errant axe blade. The incident is purely accidental, without any malice aforethought, but the neighbor dies from his injuries. Given the customs of that time, it would perhaps not have been unusual for the relatives of the deceased to seek revenge for the killing of their loved one, even though the death was strictly unintended. Under these circumstances the person whose axe flew off the handle would flee into a city of refuge, where he would be assured safety from any who might seek his life. (See Deuteronomy 19:4–6.)

These six cities of refuge included Kedesh, Shechem, and

Hebron on the west side of the Jordan River, and Bezer, Ramoth, and Golan on the east side (see Joshua 20:7–8), and a person could find a safe haven in one of these cities "unto the death of the high priest" (Numbers 35:25). It was assumed that, with the passage of time, the hearts of friends and relatives of the deceased would gradually be softened so that the fugitive's life would no longer be in jeopardy, nor would anyone else be inclined to commit an act of vengeance in a moment of anger. (See Numbers 35:26–28.)

On those days when the fiery darts of the adversary appear to overtake us or it seems that in the colosseum of life the lions are about to devour the Christians, it may be desirable for us to retreat to a city of refuge, if you will. Our safe haven may vary from person to person and from one set of circumstances to another, but it is always comforting to know that there is a place close at hand that will shelter us with security and safety from the storms of life. Following are some of these safe havens to which we may flee whenever the need arises.

The Family

Elder Henry B. Eyring has provided some profound insights into the September 1995 document "The Family: A Proclamation to the World" which was issued by the First Presidency and Council of the Twelve Apostles of The Church of Jesus Christ of Latter-day Saints. In this sacred document the Brethren "solemnly proclaim that marriage between a man and a woman is ordained of God and that the family is central to the Creator's plan for the eternal destiny of His children." Commenting upon this declaration, Elder Eyring wrote:

> Try to imagine yourself as a little child, hearing those words for the first time, and believing that they are true. . . . A little child would feel safe hearing the words that marriage between a man and woman is ordained of God. The child would know that the longing to have the love of both a father and a mother, distinct but somehow perfectly

complementary, exists because that is the eternal pattern, the pattern of happiness. The child would also feel safer knowing that God would help mother and father resolve differences and love each other, if only they will ask for his help and try. Prayers of children across the earth would go up to God, pleading for his help for parents and for families. (Henry B. Eyring, *To Draw Closer to God*, [Salt Lake City: Deseret Book Co., 1997], pp. 159–60.)

Elder Marlin K. Jensen has also described the key ingredients of living "after the manner of happiness" (2 Nephi 5:27). Sharing a personal heart petal with the youth of Zion, he said: "Sometimes after an enjoyable family home evening, or during a fervent family prayer, or when our entire family is at the dinner table on Sunday evening eating waffles and engaging in a session of lively, good-natured conversation, I quietly say to myself: 'If heaven is nothing more than this, it will be good enough for me!' " (Marlin K. Jensen, "Living After the Manner of Happiness," *BYU Devotional Speeches of the Year: 1995–96*, Provo: Brigham Young University Press, 1996, p. 30.) Would that every family were such a secure safe haven.

Ward and Branch Families

The prophet Elisha had counseled the king of Israel how to conduct war with the Syrians, and when this fact came to light the king of Syria sought to capture Elisha. When the king learned that Elisha was in the city of Dothan, he ordered a great host of horses and chariots to circle the city at night. The next morning when Elisha's servant arose, he observed that they were under siege and excitedly asked Elisha: "Alas, my master! how shall we do?" Elisha calmly answered: "Fear not: for *they that be with us are more than they that be with them.* And Elisha prayed, and said, Lord, I pray thee, open his eyes, that he may see. And the Lord opened the eyes of the young man; and he saw: and behold, the mountain was full of horses and chariots of fire round about Elisha." (2 Kings 6:8–17; emphasis added.) The

Lord smote the Syrian soldiers with temporary blindness, which allowed Elisha to lead them to Samaria where they were surrounded by the armies of Israel. Elisha counseled the king of Israel not to slay the Syrians but to feed them, and then to send them home, and afterward they "came no more into the land of Israel" (2 Kings 6:18–23).

Virginia H. Pearce, formerly a member of the General Presidency of the Young Women, alluded to the importance of wards and branches within the Church as places of refuge and comfort. She observed that "wards are not designed to replace the family unit, but to support the family and its righteous teachings. A ward is another place where there is enough commitment and energy to form a sort of 'safety net' family for each of us when our families cannot or do not provide all of the teaching and growing experiences we need to return to Heavenly Father." (Virginia H. Pearce, "Ward and Branch Families: Part of Heavenly Father's Plan for Us," *Ensign*, November 1993, p. 79.) When it appears that we are required to face life's dragons alone, a unified ward consisting of caring members concerned with each other's welfare may provide the comfort and assurance that "they that be with us are more than they that be with them."

In a latter-day revelation the Lord declared that the stakes of Zion "may be for a defense, and for a refuge from the storm, and from wrath when it shall be poured out without mixture upon the whole earth" (D&C 115:6). Would that every branch and ward and mission and stake were a hallowed city of refuge for the Saints of God.

As Alma invited those whom he had taught to be baptized in the waters of Mormon, he explained to them that membership in the "fold of God" involved a willingness "to mourn with those that mourn; yea, and comfort those that stand in need of comfort" (Mosiah 8:18). Caring visiting teachers are very supportive, concerned home teachers and loving neighbors are a great blessing, and a kindly bishop's comforting counsel can be extensions of the comfort received from on high. Ammon taught the people of Limhi that "God has provided a means that man, through faith, might work mighty miracles; therefore he becometh a great benefit to his fellow beings" (Mosiah 8:18). Bringing comfort to those in need of comfort is, indeed, a mighty miracle. In times of bereavement the Comforter reminds us of the covenants we have made in holy places which assure us that death and other trials and tribulations are but necessary steps in our eternal progression.

Councils and Counselors

Those who preside over wards, branches, missions, and stakes and over the quorums and auxiliaries associated with each of these units are often confronted with a steady stream of challenges. Sometimes a bishop or stake Primary president or elders quorum president may begin to feel the pangs of the loneliness of leadership as it seems their responsibilities weigh very heavily upon them. In His divine wisdom, the Lord's promise of comfort is extended to leaders through the wise reliance upon councils and counselors. After President Howard W. Hunter had been formally sustained as the President of the Church, he repeated the pledge made by one of his predecessors, President Joseph F. Smith, at the time he was sustained as President:

> I propose that my counselors and fellow Presidents in the First Presidency shall share with me in the responsibility of every act which I shall perform in this capacity. I do not propose to take the reins in my own hands to do as I please; but I propose to do as my brethren and I agree upon and as the Spirit of the Lord manifests to us. I have always held, and do hold, and trust I always shall hold, that it is wrong for one man to exercise all the authority and power of presidency in The Church of Jesus Christ of Latter-day Saints. I dare not assume such a responsibility, and I will not, so long as I can have men like these to stand by and counsel with me in the labors we have to perform and in doing all those things that shall tend to the peace, advancement and happi-

ness of the people of God and the building up of Zion." (Joseph F. Smith, Conference Report, October-November 1901, p. 82; cited in Howard W. Hunter, "Exceeding Great and Precious Promises," *Ensign*, November 1994, pp. 7–8.)

The Council of the First Presidency, the Council of the Twelve Apostles, stake and ward councils, and family councils all provide excellent safe havens, for "where no counsel is, the people fall: but in the multitude of counsellors there is safety" (Proverbs 11:14).

Sacred Groves

Following the example provided by Joseph Smith's First Vision, whenever we feel in doubt it is well for each of us to have available our own personal sacred grove into which we can retreat "unmarred from earthly care . . . and kneel in secret prayer" (Hans Henry Petersen, "Secret Prayer," *Hymns*, no. 144). There are many personal accounts of those who have received comfort in response to their prayers offered in times of great tribulation, and probably most of these, because of their sacred content, have remained a confidential legacy within a given family. President Boyd K. Packer recalled the account of Brother Joseph Millett, a faithful pioneer with a large family who, like so many others, was struggling to sustain his family. From his personal journal we read the following:

> One of my children came in and said that Brother Newton Hall's folks was out of bread, had none that day.
> I divided our flour in a sack to send up to Brother Hall. Just then Brother Hall came.
> Says I, "Brother Hall, are you out of flour?"
> "Brother Millett, we have none."
> "Well, Brother Hall, there is some in that sack. I have divided and was going to send it to you. Your children told mine that you was out."
> Brother Hall began to cry. He said he had tried others, but could not get any. He went to the cedars and prayed to the Lord, and the Lord told him to go to Joseph Millett.

"Well Brother Hall, you needn't bring this back. If the Lord sent
you for it you don't owe me for it."

You can't tell me how good it made me feel to know that the Lord
knew there was such a person as Joseph Millett. (Diary of Joseph Millett, holograph, Archives of The Church of Jesus Christ of Latter-day
Saints, Salt Lake City; cited in Boyd K. Packer, "A Tribute to the Rank
and File of the Church," *Ensign*, May 1980, p. 63.)

Our sacred grove may be like Newton Hall's woods of cedar
trees or merely a quiet corner in a cozy cottage, but the principle and the promises are the same: "The effectual fervent prayer
of a righteous [woman or man, girl or boy] availeth much"
(James 5:16).

Ordinances Manifest the Power of Godliness

Elder Henry B. Eyring observed that "every covenant with
God is an opportunity to draw closer to him" (Henry B. Eyring,
Transcript of CES Fireside for College-Age Young Adults,
Satellite Broadcast, September 6, 1996, p. 2). Ordinances are
outward signs of our covenants with our Heavenly Father and
His promises to us (Ibid., p. 1). The Lord has revealed that it is
in the ordinances of the priesthood that "the power of godliness
is manifest" to men in the flesh (D&C 84:19–21). Whenever
we participate in priesthood ordinances heaven and earth are
drawn into closer proximity as the "vain and foolish things of
the world" pale in importance and the things of eternity assume
their rightful place in our order of personal priorities.

We testify to the world that the prophet Elijah appeared to
Joseph Smith and Oliver Cowdery in the Kirtland Temple on the
third day of April 1836 and restored the keys of the sealing power.
These glorious keys assure that families can be forever, that love
within the family circle can transcend the bounds of death. The
spirit of Elijah supersedes those chilling words "until death you
do part" pronounced at the conclusion of many marriage cere-
monies performed in the world. The Comforter supplants the

words spoken at many a grave side, "earth to earth, ashes to ashes and dust to dust," as the bereaved look at each other with glassy eyes and ask themselves, Is this all there is to life on earth?

In holy temples married couples are promised that, upon conditions of personal worthiness, their marriage will remain intact, and their family and their posterity will increase, throughout the eternities. These promises are a wonderful source of comfort to any and all who wish to claim them through participating in the priesthood ordinances of the restored gospel. Elder Russell M. Nelson has observed that "before embarking on any journey, we like to have some assurance of a round-trip ticket. Returning from earth to life in our heavenly home requires passage through—and not around—the doors of death. We were born to die, and we die to live. (See 2 Corinthians 6:9.) As seedlings of God, we barely blossom on earth; we fully flower in heaven." (Russell M. Nelson, "Doors of Death," *Ensign*, May 1992, p. 72.)

At the heart and core of all gospel ordinances is the miracle of forgiveness, made possible by the atonement of Jesus Christ (see HC 3:30). Also at the heart of every ordinance is a manifestation of comfort from on high. Surely no one who has received the ordinances of the gospel would ever consciously refuse to be comforted. Each week as we partake of the sacramental emblems we renew our covenants with our Eternal Father, allowing us to claim the commensurate promise that we "may always have his Spirit to be with [us]" (D&C 20:77, 79). When those who have been sealed in the house of the Lord lose a loved one in death, they can claim the promise of comfort through the constant companionship of the Holy Ghost (see D&C 121:45–46) and they can proclaim with assuredness: "O death, where is thy sting? O grave, where is thy victory?" (I Corinthians 15:55.) The Prophet Joseph Smith declared that "when a seal is put upon the father and mother, it secures their posterity, so that they cannot be lost, but will be saved by virtue of the covenant of their father and mother" (HC 5:530).

The Temple Is a Place of Healing

On one occasion I attended an evening session in the Swiss Temple. Just before the session began, several cars arrived from northern Italy filled with faithful Saints from the cities of Venice, Turin, Milan, and their surrounding communities. Whenever I have visited stake conferences or other meetings in Italy I have always been impressed by the warmth and friendliness of the Saints. They always seem to be so animated and enthusiastic about life. But this Friday evening they entered the temple looking battle-weary and worn down and subdued by the cares of the world. There seemed to be more than just the effects of the three- or four-hour drive to the temple and more than just physical fatigue. They seemed to be preoccupied with their burdens.

At the conclusion of the session, as I entered the celestial room, I anticipated a lot of animated whispering accompanied by rapid hand gestures, as the Italians are accustomed to do. But on this particular evening every single head was bowed in personal prayer, and those heads remained reverently bowed for a very long time. Early the next morning we met in the chapel, where I was asked to speak briefly to these wonderful Saints prior to the first session of the day. As I looked into that sea of bright eyes and smiling faces they did not seem to be the same group of Saints I had greeted at the door the previous evening. Then, as I beheld their Christ-like countenances, the revelation came to me: The temple is not just a place of *sealing*, but it is also a place of *healing*.

President James E. Faust observed that "Our temples provide a sanctuary where we may go to lay aside many of the anxieties of the world. Our temples are places of peace and tranquillity. In these hallowed sanctuaries God 'healeth the broken in heart, and bindeth up their wounds' (Psalm 147:3)." (James E. Faust, "Spiritual Healing," *Ensign*, May 1992, p. 7.)

Those great Italian Saints had arrived battle-scarred and wounded from the daily wars of life, but in the house of the

Lord they had been healed. After participating in back-to-back endowment sessions prior to their departure for home, the feet of those Saints barely touched the ground.

The Sabbath

Several years ago, when our children were very young, we had a family home evening discussion about the pioneers and their faithful devotion to the gospel, which helped them transcend the hardships of leaving their homes and crossing the plains in wagons and with handcarts. We then sang that poignant Primary song "Pioneer Children Sang as They Walked." As I looked at our own children as they sang, I wondered how those pioneer children could have survived the endless miles of sand, sagebrush, snakes, and snow. And then came the answer in the words of the song: "Sundays they camped and read and prayed." (Elizabeth Fetzer Bates, "Pioneer Children Sang as They Walked," in *Children Sing* [Salt Lake City: The Church of Jesus Christ of Latter-day Saints, 1989], p. 214.) There was the answer. Sunday was a day of rest and refuge. The Sabbath was a safe haven from the cares of the world.

In ancient Israel the Lord repeatedly admonished his children to keep the Sabbath holy, for his Sabbaths, said he, "shall be a sign between me and you, that ye may know that I am the Lord your God" (Ezekiel 20:20). In modern revelation the Lord revealed that prayerful observance of his holy day, including participation in the sacraments, would help keep us "unspotted from the world" (D&C 59:9). There seems to be so much noise in this world from television programs and blaring radio boom boxes, and screeching jet airplanes overhead, and noisy lawn mowers next door, and eighteen-wheel trucks passing by, we have little opportunity to hear the voice of the Lord except by the still small voice. It would be well, if for at least one day a week, we could push back the noise of the world and make the Sabbath a safe haven for the Spirit in our lives.

The Spiritual Sanctuary of Fasting

Another readily available source of comfort is faithfully living the law of the fast. Much as the temple physically separates
us from the cares and fears of the secular world, fasting separates
us from the continual tug of physical appetites and insatiable
psychological needs for praise and recognition. As we subject
our bodies to our spirits, the things that matter most tend to
float to the top of our list of concerns, and we can claim the
blessings promised by the Lord through His prophet Isaiah: "Is
not this the fast that I have chosen? to loose the bands of
wickedness, to undo the heavy burdens, and to let the oppressed go free, and that ye break every yoke?" (Isaiah 58:6.) To
those who are in bondage to sins of addiction, or who carry the
heavy burdens of guilt, shame, or feelings of vengeance, and to
those who have been abused, neglected, or oppressed in any
way, the Lord has promised the breaking of *every* yoke. The
promise through the prophet Isaiah is sure: "The Lord God will
wipe away tears from off all faces" (Isaiah 25:8). The Savior rose
from the tomb "with healing in his wings" (2 Nephi 25:13). He
came "to bind up the brokenhearted . . . to comfort all that
mourn . . . [and] to give them beauty for ashes, the oil of joy for
mourning, the garment of praise for the spirit of heaviness" (Isaiah 61:1–3).

Fasting is a generally available safe haven.

The Best Books

Few places are more secure during a cold wintry storm than
when one is deeply ensconced in a comfortable chair with one
of the great books of the world; and, of course, the greatest
books are the scriptures, which invite the Spirit of the Lord into
our lives (see 1 Nephi 1:11–12; D&C 33:16). The scriptures
have been likened to "wells of salvation" out of which we can
draw the living water of the gospel (see 2 Nephi 22:3). In latter-

day revelation the Savior has declared that the scriptures "are not of men nor of man, but of me. . . . For it is my voice which speaketh them unto you; for they are given by my Spirit unto you . . . Wherefore, you can testify that you have heard my voice, and know my words." (D&C 18:34–36.) As we "feast upon the words of Christ" and "liken all scriptures" unto ourselves, "the words of Christ will tell [us] all things what [we] should do" (2 Nephi 32:3–5; 1 Nephi 19:23).

When we sometimes feel overwhelmed by our callings in the Church and painfully realize how far short we fall in fulfilling our callings, we can take some comfort from the Lord's words to Joseph Smith after he had lost the first 116 pages of the Book of Mormon manuscript: "repent of that which thou hast done which is contrary to the commandment which I gave you, and thou art still chosen, and art again called to the work" (D&C 3:10).

It is perfectly normal to have an occasional twinge of anxiety about children and grandchildren while we or they are serving a mission in faraway places. However, we can receive great comfort from the Lord's promise that "every one that hath forsaken houses, or brethren, or sisters, or father, or mother, or wife, or children, or lands, for my name's sake, shall receive an hundredfold, and shall inherit everlasting life" (Matthew 19:29). In the spirit of likening the scriptures unto ourselves, parents and other missionaries who are far from home on the Lord's errand can also claim the Lord's assurance to Sidney Rigdon and the Prophet Joseph that "your families are well; they are in mine hands, and I will do with them as seemeth me good; for in me there is all power" (D&C 100:1).

To those whose testimony sometimes seems to waver a bit, the scriptures can bring great comfort, as the revelation did to Oliver Cowdery during his labors as Joseph's scribe during the translation of the Book of Mormon in April of 1829. Said the Lord to Oliver: "Verily, verily, I say unto you, if you desire a further witness, cast your mind upon the night that you cried unto

me in your heart, that you might know concerning the truth of
these things. Did I not speak peace to your mind concerning
the matter?" (D&C 6:22–23.)

And on days when we have reached the end of our rope, we
can read of the persecution of Alma's flock of recently baptized
members at the hand of the ruthless Amulon who prohibited
the people from even praying aloud upon punishment of death.
So "Alma and his people did not raise their voices to the Lord
their God, but did pour out their hearts to him; and he did
know the thoughts of their hearts. And it came to pass that the
voice of the Lord came to them in their afflictions . . ." The
Lord honored the covenant they had made with him and
promised to deliver them from bondage and "ease the burdens
which are put upon your shoulders." And the Lord "did
strengthen them that they could bear up their burdens with
ease, and they did submit cheerfully and with patience to all the
will of the Lord." (Mosiah 24:11–15.)

There may be times when Satan plays mind games with us,
trying to convince us that our list of sins is so long that we
might as well give up trying to be obedient to the commandments of a loving Father in Heaven. Or, Lucifer may induce
undue anxiety about our standing before the Lord. These feelings are not uncommon, for Joseph Smith himself revealed that
he shared these same concerns the evening when he fervently
prayed and later was visited by the Angel Moroni. (See Joseph
Smith History—1:28–30.)

In late 1835, Brother Lyman Sherman approached the
Prophet Joseph somewhat anxious about his standing before the
Lord. Through Joseph the Lord admonished Lyman to "let your
soul be at rest concerning your spiritual standing, and resist no
more my voice. . . . Therefore, strengthen your brethren in all
your conversation, in all your prayers, in all your exhortations,
and in all your doings. . . . I am with you to bless you and deliver you forever. Amen." (D&C 108:2, 7–8.)

Whenever we become unduly anxious about our personal

spiritual standing before the Lord, we would do well to read King Benjamin's address, in which we are given several indicators that manifest that we have received and retained a remission of sins. These indicators include some of the following benchmarks: We are "filled with joy," and have a "peace of conscience," and experience "great joy in [our] souls." We are "filled with the love of God" and do "not have a mind to injure one another" nor allow our children to "transgress the laws of God, and fight and quarrel one with another." We are also inclined to "succor those that stand in need of [our] succor" and to "impart of the substance that [we] have one to another." And, in summary, "we have no more disposition to do evil, but to do good continually." (Mosiah 4:3–27; 5:2.)

Hymns of Zion

On many occasions I have found that singing and playing the hymns of Zion has provided a great safe haven in the midst of a storm. Several years ago, when I was wrestling with a particularly dark feeling of discouragement, I sat down at the piano and began to sing and play various sacrament hymns. By the end of the third hymn I felt much better, and three more hymns after that I felt the return of some sunshine in my soul. Just then the phone rang, and it was a mission president asking for help with a young man who was discouraged and homesick and who wanted to take the next plane home. I shared my experience of singing hymns with the mission president, who happened to play the piano and was a pretty good singer. I suggested he might sit down at the piano with the discouraged elder and sing a few sacrament hymns with him. He said he would call back and report the results of his experiment with the hymns of Zion. Next morning he called to report that the hymns of the Restoration had touched the young man's heart and had rekindled his faith and his desire to remain on his mission and to serve the Lord.

If the Lad Be Not with Me

One of the responsibilities of home teachers and visiting teachers and of all members of a community of Saints is to follow the admonition that as we have been comforted in all our tribulation by the God of comfort, it is then incumbent upon each of us "to comfort them which are in any trouble, by the comfort wherewith we ourselves are comforted of God" (2 Corinthians 1:3–4). This is an extension of the Savior's commandment to love one another as he has loved us (see John 15:12).

One summer two American tourists, a husband and wife, visited the South Rim of the Grand Canyon. Against their better judgment, they were persuaded to hike down the Bright Angel Trail leading to the bottom of the canyon. It was a beautiful mid-July day as they descended the trail, and although the Arizona weather was predictably very warm, they had taken with them some snacks and plenty of water to sustain themselves along the way.

Going down was not too strenuous, but climbing back up the trail began to tax their endurance. As restless, billowy white stratocumulus clouds suddenly began to change from pure white to gray, they began to hope that perhaps a few drops of rain might fall to refresh them along the way. All too soon their wish was granted as giant drops of rain began to fall upon the dusty trail. Suddenly the gray clouds turned black, and within minutes the sheer walls of the Grand Canyon began to reverberate from the deafening sound of thunder.

The spectacular display of lightning overhead was both beautiful and frightening, because each lightning bolt was immediately followed by resounding thunder that shook the walls of that vast canyon. The dusty trail soon turned to a little river of mud, and the rain turned to hail. Together with some tourists from New Jersey, Michigan, Austria, and Sweden, they ran for cover inside a short tunnel that had been carved out of the canyon wall and protected perhaps ten feet of the trail. The entire trail had now become a growing mudslide running through the tunnel, so they desperately clung onto the sides of the tunnel to keep from being swept on down the trail. Suddenly the mud slide increased in velocity and volume augmented by gravel washed from the sides of the canyon by the torrential rain and hail.

A family from Sweden were standing at the upper end of the tunnel, while the American husband and wife were standing at the lower end knee deep in mud and gravel. In the middle of the narrow trail the mud and gravel flowed much faster than around the edges. All of a sudden a young Swedish boy was caught up in the muddy current heading for the edge of the trail, which dropped about two hundred feet to the switchback below. As the last person just inside the tunnel, the American reached out and grabbed the Swedish lad and pulled him back just before he could go over the precipice. The American wife clung to her husband, lest he too be swept over the edge.

The mud and gravel slide continued churning against their legs trying to force everyone over the edge. The American woman was literally stuck in the mud up to her knees, and so she held onto her husband while he in turn held onto the young Swedish lad. The force of the slide became extremely menacing, and everyone prayed for a tempering of the elements that they might not be swept over the edge of the trail. Within seconds the mudslide suddenly became diverted further up the trail, and all the temporary inhabitants of the tunnel breathed a collective sigh of relief.

As they began to dig each other out of the mud with their hands, the father of the Swedish boy approached the older American man filled with emotion. "Thanks for saving my son," he said, "I tried so very hard, but I just couldn't reach him." As they hiked to the top of the canyon together, twice more he repeated the phrase: "I tried so very hard, but I just couldn't reach him."

The mudslide damaged the trail so badly that this particular section of the Grand Canyon was closed to tourists for several weeks to allow workers to repair and rebuild the trail. That afternoon will remain unforgettable to the two Americans, not so much because of the terror they all felt, nor because of the discomfort from the chilling rain and hail, but because of that concerned father who loved his young son so very much and tried so hard but could not reach him.

Throughout the world and within the Church there are concerned parents with children whose lives are dangerously near the precipice. These loving parents often try very hard, but because of geographical or emotional or spiritual distance they are unable to reach their children. How grateful we are when a caring Young Women's advisor, or an Aaronic Priesthood advisor, or a concerned member of a bishopric, or a sensitive seminary teacher, or faithful home teachers and devoted visiting teachers reach out and hold onto children of every age and help keep them from falling over the edge.

Our thoughts revert back to the second visit of Joseph's brothers when they returned to Egypt to procure grain, inasmuch as there was a famine in their homeland. Because of Joseph's lengthy absence from his family as a youth, his brothers did not recognize him, and when he beheld his younger brother, Benjamin, he was so delighted that "he sought where to weep; and he entered into his chamber, and wept there. And he washed his face, and went out, and refrained himself" from disclosing his true identity (Genesis 43:30–31.) After feasting with his brethren, Joseph then gave orders to fill their sacks with food and to return their money to them. With an intriguing motive in mind he also instructed his servants secretly to put his personal silver cup in "the sack's mouth of the youngest," his brother Benjamin (Genesis 44:2).

After his brethren had departed Joseph asked his steward to follow them and to search the sacks they had taken with them. In accordance with Joseph's plan, the silver cup was discovered in Benjamin's sack. His brothers returned to Joseph's house and "fell before him on the ground" placing themselves at his mercy. Maintaining a sober countenance, Joseph stated that "the man in whose hand the cup is found, he shall be my servant," and he commanded the rest of the brothers to return in peace to their father (Genesis 44:1–17.) It was at this point that Judah protectively tried to intercede in behalf of young Benjamin, saying: "We have a father, an old man, and a child of his old age, a little one; and his brother is dead, and he alone is left of his mother, and his father loveth him" (Genesis 44:18–20.) Judah reminded Joseph of the first visit of the ten brothers when they had left Benjamin behind on the grounds that "The lad [could not] leave his father: for if he should leave his father, his father would die." Joseph had, on that first occasion, insisted that his older brothers bring Benjamin with them on their next visit. Failing that, Joseph would not show his face again. (Genesis 44:23–34; 43:5.)

Judah explained to Joseph that if they were to return to their father Jacob without their young brother "when he seeth that the lad is not with us . . . he will die" (Genesis 44:31). Then, in an act of supernal unselfishness, Judah offered to remain and be Joseph's servant in the place of Benjamin, saying: "For *how shall I go up to my father, and the lad be not with me?*" (Genesis 44:33–34; emphasis added.)

There are many fathers and mothers in Zion who agonize over their sons and daughters who presently seem indifferent to spiritual things. In anguish their prayers ascend heavenward as they ask the introspective question: How shall we go up to our Father in Heaven, and our son or daughter be not with us?

Elder John K. Carmack cautions the parents of wayward children that "Because our children follow a different course than we have taught them does not give us license to reject them." They still deserve our continuous love and prayers and moral support. He counsels parents to continue to trust their Father in Heaven and to turn to the Savior, to respect the moral agency of their children, to refrain from unrighteous judgment, and, very important, to never give up on their children. He further counsels parents not to "unwisely place their own personal hopes and dreams on the achievement of their children," and reminds parents that "often there are others who have greater influence in your children's lives than you do during troubled times." (John K. Carmack, "When Our Children Go Astray," *Ensign*, February 1997, pp. 8–12.) Sometimes that indifferent daughter or spiritually neutral son will respond to the loving invitation of a bishop, a concerned neighbor, a grandparent, aunt, uncle, or exemplary business associate who gently leads them to a spiritual safe haven far from the fiery darts of the adversary.

God bless all of the Saints of the Most High who reach out to the wayward sons and daughters, not their own, and who follow the admonition of Paul in comforting others "by the comfort wherewith [they themselves] are comforted of God" (2 Corinthians 1:3–4) and who abide by Alma's admonition to "bear one another's burdens, that they may be light . . . to mourn with those that mourn; yea, and comfort those that stand in need of comfort" (Mosiah 18:8–9).

The exhortation to render comfort to others is but an extension of the two great commandments—to love the Lord and to love our neighbors as ourselves (see Matthew 22:36–39). To those in need of comfort and to those who mourn, the peace provided by the Comforter and the comfort from caring home teachers, visiting teachers, and other friends and neighbors is of inestimable worth and a confirmation of the Savior's promise: "Peace I leave with you, my peace I give unto you: not as the world giveth, give I unto you. Let not your heart be troubled, neither let it be afraid." (John 14:27.)

Where Can I Turn for Peace?

Where can I turn for peace?
Where is my solace
When other sources cease to make me whole?
When with a wounded heart, anger, or malice,
I draw myself apart,
Searching my soul?

Where, when my aching grows,
Where, when I languish,
Where, in my need to know, where can I run?
Where is the quiet hand to calm my anguish?
Who, who can understand?
He, only One.

He answers privately,
Reaches my reaching
In my Gethsemane, Savior and Friend.
Gentle the peace he finds for my beseeching.
Constant he is and kind,
Love without end.

(Emma Lou Thayne, *Hymns*, No. 129.)

FOUR

Enter into the Rest
of the Lord

THE GOSPEL OF JESUS CHRIST CONTAINS AN occasional, apparent paradox such as the Savior's statement that "He that findeth his life shall lose it: and he that loseth his life for my sake shall find it" (Matthew 10:39; see also Luke 9:24). To some, this paradox may appear to be irreconcilable, but to those who have foregone the immediate pleasures of retirement to accept the rigorous challenges and blessings of missionary service, temple work, or family history research, or who continually extend themselves in comforting others, there is a great understanding and appreciation for the Savior's teaching. For those who continue the pursuit of ever-elusive pleasures, the Savior's statement remains an enigma.

Another apparent paradox is contained in the numerous scriptures referring to "the rest of the Lord" when juxtaposed with the Lord's own declaration that "there is no end to my works, neither to my words. For behold, this is my work and my glory—to bring to pass the immortality and eternal life of man." (Moses 1:38–39.) The question arises: If there is no end to the Lord's works, how can we speak of entering into His rest? Are not work and rest antithetical to each other?

In many passages throughout the Old Testament the Lord promises the Israelites rest from their enemies (see Deuteronomy 12:10; Joshua 21:44; Joshua 23:1; JST 2 Samuel 7:11; 2 Chronicles 14:6; 1 Kings 5:4). While a respite from war would be most welcome, the rest of the Lord encompasses much more than refuge from physical combat.

Other scriptures contain the Lord's promises to the children of Israel that they might rest from their relentless travels as they finally reach the land of promise (Joshua 1:13; 1 Kings 8:56; 1 Chronicles 23:25). But there is a kind of rest that transcends both a freedom from fighting and a freedom from fleeing, and this is the rest described so eloquently by the Savior : "Peace I leave with you, my peace I give unto you: not as the world giveth, give I unto you. Let not your heart be troubled, neither let it be afraid." (John 14:27.) The antithesis of the rest of the Lord is found in Isaiah's observation that "the wicked are like the troubled sea, when it cannot rest, whose waters cast up mire and dirt. There is no peace, saith my God, to the wicked." (Isaiah 57:20–21.)

Three Kinds of Rest

Elder Bruce R. McConkie identified three different states of rest described in the scriptures. The first is "here and now in mortality." The second state is "a more perfected rest" that accrues to the righteous who die and enter into paradise prior to their resurrection and judgment. A third, even more lasting and eternal rest is experienced by those "who have risen in immortal glory ever to be with their Lord." (Bruce R. McConkie, *The Promised Messiah* [Salt Lake City, Deseret Book, 1982], p. 318.)

Rest in the Present Time

The Apostle Paul promised the Hebrews that those who believed the word of God would enter into His rest, whereas those who hardened their hearts would not enter into His rest because "the word did not profit them, not being mixed with faith in them that heard it" (JST Hebrews 4:1–3). The prophet Mormon underscored the accessibility of the Lord's rest while in mortality as he declared: "I would speak unto you that are of the church, that are the peaceable followers of Christ, and that have obtained a sufficient hope by which ye can enter into the rest of the Lord, from this time henceforth until ye shall rest with him in heaven" (Moroni 7:3). Elaborating upon this passage of scripture, President Joseph F. Smith taught: "The rest here referred to is not physical rest, for there is no such thing as physical rest in the Church of Jesus Christ. Reference is made to the spiritual rest and peace which are born from a settled conviction of the truth in the minds of men. We may thus enter into the rest of the Lord today, by coming to an understanding of the truths of the gospel. No people is more entitled to this rest—this peace of the spirit—than are members of the Church." (Joseph F. Smith, *Gospel Doctrine*, [Salt Lake City: Deseret Book, 1989], p. 126.)

President Spencer W. Kimball, who gave us the watchwords "lengthen your stride" and "quicken your pace," reemphasized the foregoing distinction between the Lord's rest and physical rest. Said President Kimball: "Sometimes we have thought of rest as being a place where we get on the chaise lounge, or in our sneakers, or we get outside and lie on the grass, something where we are at rest. That isn't the kind of rest that the Lord is speaking about. It is he who is the most dynamic, the one who works the hardest, puts in the longest hours, and lives closest to his Heavenly Father who is rested—rested from his labors, but not put away from his work." (Spencer W. Kimball, "The Privilege of Holding the Priesthood, *Ensign*, November 1975, p. 80.)

Elder Wilford Woodruff also disclosed his sense of urgency for the Lord's work: "I think, many times, that we, as Elders of Israel and as Latter-day Saints, come far short of realizing our position before the Lord. The work required at our hands is great and mighty; it is the work of Almighty God. We are held responsible for presenting the Gospel of Christ to all the nations of the earth, to warn the Gentiles, to prepare for the return of the lost ten tribes of Israel, and for carrying the Gospel to the whole tribes of Israel. We are held responsible for all this, and for building Temples to the Most High, wherein we can enter and attend to ordinances for the salvation of our dead." (*Journal of Discourses*, 18:114.) In light of the foregoing remarks of President Woodruff and President Kimball, it may be that unreliable home teachers, and missionaries who sleep late every morning, just *think* they are at rest.

Headwinds and Tailwinds of Life

Some time ago Elders Cecil O. Samuelson, Jr. and John E. Fowler and I found ourselves in the Oslo, Norway, Airport anxiously awaiting the late arrival of an airplane that was to fly us to Denmark. Meetings had been scheduled to begin shortly after our arrival, so we became quite apprehensive when our plane failed to arrive on time. Eventually we saw the plane pierce the clouds and finally approach the gate at the terminal.

After all the passengers were seated and ready for take-off, we heard the pilot's voice on the loudspeaker: "Ladies and gentlemen, we apologize for our late arrival in Oslo. However, we have some good news and some bad news. The bad news is that we were delayed by a strong northerly headwind on our way here from Denmark. The good news is that we will be the beneficiaries of a strong southerly tailwind as we return to Denmark. In fact, with this strong tailwind, we expect to land just about on time." Notwithstanding our apprehensions, thanks to the strong tailwind we were able to arrive punctually at our meeting.

Since that occasion I have thought a lot about the headwinds and tailwinds in our lives. Father Lehi explained to his son Jacob that there must be opposition in all things in our lives (see 2 Nephi 2:11). He did not say there *might* be opposition, or there *could* be opposition, or even that there *would* be opposition in all things; Lehi said there *must* be opposition in *all* things. For every tailwind there is a commensurate headwind, and when the winter weather is bitter cold we especially prefer to have the wind at our back.

As I look into the hopeful faces of the youth of Zion and as I meet with many adult members whose lives have been marred by the ongoing troubles of life, I think of the impact of headwinds and tailwinds. The Lord declared that "he who is faithful and wise in time is accounted worthy to inherit the mansions prepared for him of my Father" (D&C 72:4). There is the young man in high school who does not avail himself of the opportunity to take seminary classes and he avoids bracing himself against the headwinds of challenging academic courses that would prepare him for further vocational training or a university education. He avoids the exhilarating headwind of a mission call. Instead, he takes a job at a minimum pay level upon graduation from school. Rather than investing money for additional education and vocational training he prefers the immediate gratification of earning money. He prefers watching television to reading good books that would improve his mind and his skills. He takes out a loan for a new car, but the interest on his monthly payments and his insurance payments consume almost all that he makes. After a few years, with little or no money saved, he falls in love and wishes to marry. He and his girlfriend reason that if both of them keep working they can pool their resources and make ends meet. Ten years and three children later they never seem to have an extra penny to their name, and money becomes a source of continual contention in their relationship.

President Gordon B. Hinckley has exhorted the youth of Zion: "Get all the education you can. I repeat, I do not care what you want to be as long as it is honorable. A car mechanic, a bricklayer, a plumber, an electrician, a doctor, a lawyer, a merchant, but not a thief. But whatever you are, take the opportunity to train for it and make the best of that opportunity. Society will reward you according to your worth as it perceives that worth. Now is the great day of preparation for each of you. If it means sacrifice, then sacrifice. That sacrifice will become the best investment you have ever made, for you will reap returns from it all the days of your lives." (Eugene Oregon Regional Conference, September 15, 1996.)

There is the young woman, age sixteen, whose parents and teachers have taught her the importance of living a chaste and pure life in preparation for a temple marriage. But the law of chastity can seem to some young people like a blustery, unwelcome headwind that merely spoils the pleasures of life. She and her boyfriend are in love, and no one is going to ruin their lives with preachy old-fashioned values. In an unguarded moment they express their affection beyond the bounds of propriety, and though she was certain her boyfriend loved her and would marry her, they both suddenly realize he is in no position to support a family. His parents move across the country in an attempt to avoid the shame he has brought upon their family, and she is left alone with a new baby. After discussing the matter with her parents and bishop, she places the child with an adoption agency, at least providing a source of joy to a young couple unable to have children. But her self-esteem is badly damaged, her relationship with her parents is strained, and her relationship with her Heavenly Father needs to be strengthened.

Reminding young Latter-day Saints to honor parents and to accept their counsel, President Hinckley said: "No one has a greater interest in your welfare, in your happiness, in your future than do your mothers and fathers. They are of a prior generation. That is true. But they were once the age that you are now. Your problems are not substantially different from what theirs were. If they occasionally place restrictions on you, it is because they see danger down the road. Listen to them. What they ask you to do may not be to your liking. But you will be much happier if you do it." ("Stand True and Faithful," *Ensign*, May 1996, pp. 92–93.)

Many of the younger generation perceive the Word of Wisdom to be an especially strong headwind in their lives, especially when their popularity seems to be at stake if they do not participate in experimenting with drugs, tobacco, and alcohol. Little do they realize that the Word of Wisdom is much, much more than a code of health. President Boyd K. Packer exhorted all of us to avoid the use of addictive substances because they "interfere with the delicate feelings of spiritual communication [which] may cost you the 'great treasures of knowledge, even hidden treasures' " (Boyd K. Packer, "Personal Revelation: The Gift, the Test, and the Promise," *Ensign*, November 1994, p. 61).

Withstanding temptation to partake of tea, coffee, tobacco, alcohol, and any other form of drugs may constitute a rather brisk headwind in the lives of some of the youth of today. However, it is a far better thing to withstand the temporary headwind of peer-group pressure and possible ostracism now than to face the even stronger headwinds throughout an entire lifetime as addictions increase in strength while the physical body is enslaved and becomes emaciated, and the freedom of choice is held hostage. I have yet to meet a person with emphysema who extols the virtues of smoking, and I have never met a victim of cirrhosis of the liver who argues in behalf of the benefits of drinking alcohol. The Word of Wisdom helps protect one of God's greatest gifts—moral agency, the freedom to choose.

Young people who lean into the headwinds of challenging courses in public school, in trade schools and colleges and universities, generally reap the harvest of several tailwinds later in life. Faithfully foregoing a precious hour of extra sleep in order to attend early-morning seminary will reap a rich harvest later on. Not only will the harvester be able to drink deeply from a well of gospel knowledge but also the self-discipline gained from taking seminary will also serve well when he or she is faced with challenging occupational opportunities. Those who deliver newspapers in torrential rain or arctic snow, or who milk two dozen cows twice a day, or who babysit or work at a part-time job after school will all be well equipped to face many of life's future challenges.

That is not to say there will not be other challenges, disappointments, and growth experiences, but youth who have faced the headwinds are in a far better position to meet those challenges than are those who invariably take the path of least resistance, always preferring tailwinds to headwinds. A constant diet of watching videos or television or listening to hard rock music on a boom box does little to prepare anyone for anything. C. S. Lewis wrote: "Only those who try to resist temptation know how strong it is. . . . You find out the strength of a wind by trying to walk against it, not by lying down" (*Mere Christianity* [New York: Macmillan Co., 1960], p. 124). It takes considerably more effort to read great books than to watch television, but the effort will continually provide a rich harvest throughout one's life. A regular physical exercise program may constitute a rather stiff headwind now, but the long-term consequences can hardly be over-emphasized.

Couples who meticulously live the law of chastity and marry in the house of the Lord will not automatically live lives free from chilling headwinds, but they will be the recipients of added spiritual strength to meet those challenges. After being sealed in the temple they will have that persistent, quiet assurance, when experiencing serious illness or imminent death, that their family is forever. In moments of disagreement and occasional contention, they will always stop short of open conflict and will strive for rapid reconciliation as they remember the sacred covenants they have made in the temple to their Heavenly Father and to each other.

The Lord promises that "they who have sought me early shall find rest to their souls" (D&C 54:10). Withstanding the headwinds of temptation and leaning into the headwinds of the challenging years of preparation during mortality will prepare us for the tailwinds of eternity, when we shall "hie to Kolob in the twinkling of an eye" (William W. Phelps, *Hymns*, no. 284).

Rest Through Repentance

In exhorting the Saints of his day to repent and "enter into the rest of God," Alma spoke of the days of Melchizedek, a righteous king in the land of Salem, who preached repentance so effectively that many of his followers became "sanctified by the Holy Ghost, having their garments made white, being pure and spotless before God." Alma then provided one of the hallmarks of sanctification, and that is they "could not look upon sin save it were with abhorrence" and they "were made pure and entered into the rest of the Lord their God." (Alma 13:11–17.) Righteousness and rest reinforce each other. When one looks upon sin with abhorrence one is invariably at rest when faced with a given temptation. One does not waste needless energy or effort in deciding whether to go to an R-rated movie, or whether to go to a ball game on Sunday, or whether to pay a full tithing, or whether to drink a martini at a business luncheon with the boss. Someone at rest has already made those decisions well in advance, and those at rest generally have friends and associates who understand how these decisions will be made in advance.

President Joseph F. Smith observed that, in contrast to those at rest, there are many other people who "are driven about by every wind of doctrine, thus being ill at ease, unsettled, restless. These are they who are discouraged over incidents that occur in the Church, and in the nation, and in the turmoils of men and associations. They harbor a feeling of suspicion, unrest, uncertainty. Their thoughts are disturbed, and they become excited with the least change, like one at sea who has lost his bearings." (Ibid.) Sometimes we find it easier to sustain a belief in continuing revelation than it is to accept change when, in fact, continuing revelation often leads to change, and, generally, change for the better in our personal lives.

Although the Lord admonishes us to "be anxiously engaged in a good cause" (D&C 58:27), Elder Neal A. Maxwell cautions us against becoming so overly-anxious we then become "hectically engaged" (*Men and Women of Christ* [Salt Lake City: Bookcraft, 1991], p. 24). He further observed that "the disciple should be anxiously engaged and watchful, but he need not be filled with overanxiety to the point of lessened effectiveness" (*Wherefore Ye Must Press Forward* [Salt Lake City: Deseret Book, 1977], p. 63). This was a personal concern of Nephi's brother Jacob, who confessed the hope that he would not "get shaken from [his] firmness in the Spirit, and stumble because of [his] over anxiety" for those for whom he had responsibility (see Jacob 4:18).

President Brigham Young exhorted the Saints of the previous century not to be "too anxious for the Lord to hasten his work. Let our anxiety be centered upon this one thing, the sanctification of our own hearts, the purifying of our own affections, the preparing of ourselves for the approach of the events that are hastening upon us. This should be our concern, this should be our study, this should be our daily prayer, and not to be in a hurry to see the overthrow of the wicked." (*Journal of Discourses* 9:3.)

Many of our anxieties are rooted in pride, which President Ezra Taft Benson described as "the great stumbling block in Zion." President Benson taught that "Most of us think of pride as self-centeredness, conceit, boastfulness, arrogance, or haughtiness. All of these are elements of the sin, but the heart, or core, is still missing.

"The central feature of pride is enmity—enmity toward God and enmity toward our fellowmen. . . . Pride is essentially competitive in nature. We pit our will against God's. When we direct our pride toward God, it is in the spirit of 'my will and not thine be done'. . . . The proud make every man their adversary by pitting their intellects, opinions, works, wealth, talents, or any other worldly measuring device against others. In the words of C. S. Lewis: 'Pride gets no pleasure out of having something, only out of having more of it than the next man. . . . It is the comparison that makes you proud: the pleasure of being above the rest. Once the element of competition has gone, pride has gone.' (*Mere Christianity* [New York: Macmillan, 1952], pp. 109–10.)" (Ezra Taft Benson, "Beware of Pride," *Ensign*, May, 1989, p. 4.)

The proud are seldom at rest with themselves or with the Lord, because there is always some other less worthy person overtaking their position in the pecking order of life.

The Super-Mom Syndrome

For many years it was predominantly members of the male gender who were engaged in fierce athletic competition on the playing field and economic competition in the marketplace, but times are changing. Women now compete in a wide variety of track and field events, swimming, ice skating, and a host of other athletic events, and in the occupational world they are assuming ever-increasing prominence in the professions and managerial ranks. All of these changes increase the pressure of competition and restlessness. But there is another kind of very subtle competition that robs many women of rest, and that is the so-called "Super-Mom Syndrome."

There is, in the minds of many women, the idyllic notion that unless a woman has jogged five miles, read five chapters in the scriptures, cleaned the house to immaculate perfection, and written five letters before the break of dawn, she does not quite measure up. All of her children must take piano or violin lessons, dancing lessons, swimming lessons, and tennis lessons, and play on the soccer team and achieve the highest scores on their school exams, or the mother has been a total and complete failure. Parents, and especially mothers, who are so driven by this compelling urge to have each and every one of their children excel in everything rob themselves and their children of rest of any kind. And those whose children *do* excel give their relatives precious little rest at family reunions. Especially appropriate for parents and children is Alma's counsel to "teach them to never be weary of good works, but to be meek and lowly in heart; for such shall find rest to their souls" (Alma 37:34).

Henry D. Eyring

One truly accomplished person whose life reflected that of a busy man at rest was the late Henry D. Eyring, the father of Elder Henry B. Eyring of the Council of the Twelve. Elder Eyring's father was a renowned professor of chemistry who had been on the faculty of Princeton University and later came to the University of Utah, where he served for many years as Dean of the Graduate School and Distinguished Professor of Chemistry. He never took a sabbatical leave, as did most other professors, who needed extra time every six years or so to refurbish their skills and "get away from it all" so they could return to the classroom refreshed. Professor Eyring's daily regimen of personal prayer, gospel study, laboratory research, teaching, and university administrative duties always kept him refreshed. He was a man at peace with himself and with the world.

When Elder Cecil O. Samuelson, Jr., was a freshman student at the University of Utah he and Professor Eyring simultaneously converged from different directions at the same drinking fountain. Brother Samuelson immediately stepped back in deference to the older Professor Eyring. The distinguished professor smiled and gestured for Cecil to drink first, saying: "Young man, please go first. I'm sure that you are busier than I am." (See Cecil O. Samuelson, Jr., "The Importance of Meekness in the Disciple-Scholar," in Henry B. Eyring, ed., *On Becoming a Disciple-Scholar* [Salt Lake City: Bookcraft, 1995], p. 54.)

Professor Eyring achieved great acclaim for his scientific contributions and numerous publications, but notwithstanding his receiving many accolades of men the Nobel Prize always eluded him. On one occasion someone asked him if he was not candidly very disappointed at not having received the coveted Nobel Prize for his significant scientific achievements. With a familiar twinkle in his eye, Professor Eyring responded, "I've awarded it to myself privately many times."

During a sophisticated lecture by a visiting scientist, Professor Eyring was asked for his reactions to the topic under discussion. He replied: "It all seems a bit too complex for me to understand. This morning I was just wondering what keeps us from dissolving while taking a shower." Here was a man at rest. First of all, his sense of humor made him superior to his circumstances, and second, he knew that, in the eternal perspective, the Nobel Prize and his scientific knowledge paled in comparison to the blessings promised by Paul's words: "Eye hath not seen, nor ear heard, neither have entered into the heart of man, the things which God hath prepared for them that love him" (I Corinthians 2:9).

Rest from Doubt and Fear

President Joseph F. Smith urged the Saints to "seek for strength from the Source of all strength, and he will provide spiritual contentment, a rest which is incomparable with the physical rest that cometh after toil. All who seek have a right to, and may enter into, the rest of God, here upon the earth, from this time forth, now, today; and when earth-life is finished, they shall also enjoy his rest in heaven." (Ibid., p. 127.) President Smith described the rest of the Lord in the here and now as "entering into the knowledge and love of God," and no longer "hunting for something else," not being disturbed "by every wind of doctrine, or by the cunning and craftiness of men who lie in wait to deceive." (Ibid., p. 58.)

One of the greatest sources of disquietude in our lives comes from the accumulation of pet peeves and an endless inventory of offenses by others. Living in close proximity with neighbors and working in close proximity with business associates and with other members of the Church in our respective ecclesiastical callings provide ample opportunities to disagree, to become disagreeable, and, on occasion, to feel offended by the inconsiderate actions of others. We deny ourselves of both physical and spiritual rest when we continue to nurture those offenses and relive them over and over again "in the compulsive musings of the day and the seething dreams of night. The moment becomes a season; the event becomes a condition." (Kai Erikson, *A New Species of Trouble: Explorations in Disaster, Trauma, and Community* [New York: W. W. Norton, 1994], p. 230.)

President Joseph F. Smith taught that one enters into the rest of the Lord when one "has reached that degree of faith in God that all doubt and fear have been cast from him" (Conference Report, October 1909, p. 8). "Happy is the man, indeed, " continues President Smith, "who can receive this soul-satisfying testimony, and be at rest, and seek for no other road to peace than by the doctrines of Jesus Christ" (*Gospel Doctrine*, p. 127).

The Fruit of the Spirit

The Apostle Paul taught the Galatians that "the fruit of the Spirit is love, joy, peace, longsuffering, gentleness, goodness, faith, meekness, temperance" (Galatians 5:22–23). Those who resist reconciliation will not realize peace and rest, for even the most extreme form of retribution, whether measured in lengthy prison terms or enormous monetary settlements, will never restore the peace of mind that comes from being able to forgive. The prayerful pathway to peace and rest will enable us to echo Joyce Underwood's sentiments cited in a previous chapter: "We can forgive."

Following are some of the characteristics and feelings of those at rest and those not at rest:

Those at rest are generally . . .	*Those not at rest are often . . .*
Filled with love	Sarcastic and cynical
Joyful and happy	Unhappy and miserable
Peaceful and contented	Discontented and restless
Longsuffering and patient	Impatient and anxious
Gentle and kind	Brusque and insensitive
Tolerant, forgiving and compassionate	Vengeful, unforgiving, critical
Filled with faith, hope, and optimism	Discouraged and pessimistic
Meek and humble	Proud, arrogant, harboring false aspirations
Temperate	Fanatical and overly zealous

The Apostle Paul taught the Hebrews that the word of God would not profit them unless it was "mixed with faith in them that heard it." Those who believe and live by the word will enter into the Lord's rest. (See Hebrews 4:1–3.)

Rest in Paradise

Another state of rest occurs at death, and we are not speaking here of rigor mortis. Alma taught that when we die and our spirit departs from our body, there is a state between "death and the resurrection" when "the spirits of those who are righteous are received into a state of happiness, which is called paradise, a state of rest, a state of peace, where they shall rest from all their troubles and from all care, and sorrow" (Alma 40:11–12). The degree of rest in this state will transcend the rest we may attain in this mortal sphere. However, those who "chose evil works rather than good . . . shall be cast out into outer darkness; there shall be weeping, and wailing, and gnashing of teeth, and this because of their own iniquity, being led captive by the will of the devil" (Alma 40:13). Alma dispels the belief that those who were dishonest, unkind, and unclean will, after death, suddenly become men and women of integrity, compassion, and virtue. Instead, he explains that restoration after death involves partaking "of the fruits of their labors or their works, which have been evil" (Alma 40:26; see also 40:22–25).

Rest in the Presence of God

A third state of rest is reserved for those who will, following the resurrection and judgment, enter into a more permanent, eternal rest. In the words of Elder Bruce R. McConkie, this great blessing accrues to us "after we have put our houses in order and have harmonized our lives with the doctrines that have been revealed, then we are entitled to know that this is the Lord's kingdom and to know it as a matter of faith and testimony, as a matter of feeling and revelation. Once we get that in our hearts we enter into the rest of the Lord . . . Because our testimonies are secure, we rest from all anxiety and turmoil of spirit, and if we continue in diligence and valiance in the kingdom we will eventually rest with our Father in Heaven in the eternal worlds, 'which rest is the fulness of his glory.' " (D&C 84:14; Bruce R. McConkie, Conference Report, October 1947, p. 62.)

Joseph and Hyrum Enter into the Lord's Rest

On his way to Carthage, just three days before he was assassinated, the Prophet Joseph said: "I am going like a lamb to the slaughter; but I am calm as a summer's morning; I have a conscience void of offense towards God, and towards all men" (D&C 135:4). Five years previously, as he languished in Liberty Jail, Joseph had cried out in anguish: "O God, where art thou? And where is the pavilion that covereth thy hiding place?" (D&C 121:1.) The Lord's comforting response dispelled his despair and quieted his troubled soul: "My son, peace be unto thy soul; thine adversity and thine afflictions shall be but a small moment . . . Let thy bowels also be full of charity towards all men, and to the household of faith, and let virtue garnish thy thoughts unceasingly; then shall thy confidence wax strong in the presence of God . . . [and] The Holy Ghost shall be thy constant companion . . ." (D&C 121:7, 45–46). Throughout his life the Prophet Joseph's prayers often became invitations to receive revelation and rest to his soul.

On June 28, 1844 when the bullet-riddled bodies of Hyrum and Joseph were brought from Carthage to Nauvoo, their grief-stricken mother cried in anguish: "My God, my God, why hast thou forsaken this family!" The Lord comforted her with that peace which passeth human understanding speaking to her troubled heart: "I have taken them to myself, that they might have rest." The Prophet's mother then confessed: "Oh! at that moment how my mind flew through every scene of sorrow and distress which we had passed, together, in which they had shown the innocence and sympathy which filled their guileless hearts. As I looked upon their peaceful, smiling countenances, I seemed almost to hear them say, 'Mother, weep not for us, we have overcome the world by love; we carried to them the gospel, that their souls might be saved; they slew us for our testimony, and thus placed us beyond their power; their ascendency is for a moment, ours is an eternal triumph.'

"I then thought upon the promise which I had received in Missouri, that in five years Joseph should have power over all his enemies. The time had elapsed and the promise was fulfilled." (Lucy Mack Smith, *History of Joseph Smith* [Salt Lake City: Bookcraft, 1956], p. 324.)

Joseph and Hyrum had entered into the rest of the Lord, "which rest is the fulness of his glory" (D&C 84:24). Mother Smith accepted the Savior's invitation: "Come unto me, all ye that labour and are heavy laden, and I will give you rest. . . . For my yoke is easy, and my burden is light." (Matthew 11:28, 30.)

FIVE

Rest Through Reconciliation

IN TEACHING US HOW TO ENTER INTO THE rest of the Lord while here on earth, President Joseph F. Smith reminds us "that it is better to suffer wrong than to do wrong, and to pray for our enemies and for those who despitefully use us" (*Gospel Doctrine*, p. 128). The Lord has unequivocally declared: "I, the Lord, will forgive whom I will forgive, but *of you it is required to forgive all men*" (D&C 64:10; emphasis added; see also D&C 82:23). Forgiveness of others brings rest to their souls while also providing rest to one's own soul.

A young college student from the West invited a young coed from the South to go with him for a short drive into the mountains above the college campus where both of them were furthering their education. The roads were very steep and contained several sharp curves, and the altitude increased several thousand feet over a stretch of only a few miles. They passed several cars on the way to the summit, and on their way down the mountain road the young man was driving much too fast for the steep terrain. As they rounded a sharp bend in the road the car hit the gravel shoulder and rolled over the guardrail and plunged down a ravine, eventually landing in the river at the bottom of the canyon. The young girl was killed instantly, but somehow the young man was spared any serious injury.

An ambulance and the highway patrol were called to the scene of the accident, but alas, any efforts to save the young woman were in vain. The law enforcement officials investigating the accident gathered as much evidence as possible, measuring the brake marks on the roadway, interviewing witnesses in other cars who had observed the young man's driving behavior, and so forth. The evidence pointed to reckless driving on the part of the young man, so he was arrested for his negligent behavior. Because of the preponderance of evidence, a trial was held within a few weeks of the accident.

To the surprise of all, the parents of the young woman appeared in court to plead for mercy for the young man who had caused the accident that claimed the life of their daughter. Largely because of their merciful intervention the young man was spared a prison term and was allowed to start his life anew.

The actions of the bereaved parents reflected the plea in the Lord's Prayer to "forgive us our debts as we forgive our debtors." Instead of demanding their "pound of flesh" in a court of law, they compassionately forgave the young man. By so doing, they experienced the rest of the Lord.

His Yoke Is Easy

The Savior's requirement that we forgive others becomes much easier when we accept His gentle invitation to "Come unto me, all ye that labour and are heavy laden, and I will give you rest. Take my yoke upon you, and learn of me; for I am meek and lowly in heart: and ye shall find rest unto your souls. For my yoke is easy, and my burden is light." (Matthew 11:28–30.) It is significant that a loving Savior underscores the fact that *His* yoke is easy and *His* burden is light. There are other yokes in the world which are both extremely difficult and heavy. Among these are the yokes of sin, anguish, an unforgiving heart, paranoia, pride, addictive behaviors, an unbridled tongue, discouragement, and despair.

Reconciliation with Former Foes

I was pleased to receive the assignment to dedicate a beautiful chapel in Airdrie, Scotland. The previous chapel had been maliciously burned out by some suspected youthful arsonists. Now, after about three years of waiting for the reconstruction of a new chapel, the Saints gathered at the dedicatory services with a sense of grateful anticipation. A venerable, white-haired former bishop, Bishop Forsyth, was invited to offer the invocation. It would have been irreverent of me to take notes during his prayer, but memory recalls words to this effect: ". . . and Heavenly Father, bless the young lads who burned down our chapel that their hearts might be softened toward us even as we have forgiven them of their deeds." The Spirit was very strong and sweet as each of those faithful Scottish Saints in attendance voiced a resounding "Amen" to Bishop Forsyth's prayer of reconciliation.

Reconciliation between perpetrators and victims is perhaps more challenging when it involves entire nations. In his general theory of relativity the great German physicist Albert Einstein predicted that light would bend with the pull of gravitational fields. Thus one would predict that the gravitational field of the sun would deflect the light of stars orbiting around it. The brilliant British physicist, Stephen Hawking, discussed the challenges involved in actually measuring Einstein's predictions of light deflection:

> It is normally very difficult to see this effect, because the light from the sun makes it impossible to observe stars that appear near to the sun in the sky. However, it is possible to do so during the eclipse of the sun, when the sun's light is blocked out by the moon. Einstein's prediction of light deflection could not be tested immediately in 1915, because the First World War was in progress, and it was not until 1919 that a British

expedition, observing an eclipse from West Africa, showed that light was indeed deflected by the sun, just as predicted by the theory. This proof of a German theory by British scientists was hailed as a great act of reconciliation between the two countries after the war." (Stephen Hawking, A *Brief History of Time: Updated and Expanded Edition,* [London: Bantam Press, 1996], p. 42.)

Reconciliation with Priesthood Leaders

The Apostle Paul taught the Ephesians that the Church was organized for "the perfecting of the Saints" (Ephesians 4:12), and working in a voluntary capacity in close proximity with other lay leaders can be both a wonderful blessing and also a trial of our faith. As Elder Neal A. Maxwell put it, "Life in the Church means experiencing leaders who are not always wise, mature, and deft. In fact, some of us are as bumpy and uneven as a sackful of old doorknobs. Some of the polishing we experience is a result of grinding against each other. How vital submissiveness is in such circumstances, especially if the lubrication of love is not amply present." (Neal A. Maxwell, *Not My Will, but Thine* [Salt Lake City: Bookcraft, 1988], p. 74.) The greatest disappointments during the life of the Prophet Joseph Smith were those occasions when friends he had loved and trusted turned against him. If there are those who can find fault with the Prophet of God, it should not be surprising when an occasional member feels alienated from his or her bishop or branch president.

Incidents like this have occurred for different reasons in various cultures since the beginning of time. One of the great figures of the Book of Mormon is Pahoran, who had been severely castigated and even threatened by Captain Moroni who, with inadequate information, incorrectly assumed that Pahoran was deleterious in discharging his civic duties and responsibilities as chief judge and governor. Pahoran's magnanimity is reflected in his reponse to Moroni's chastening epistle: "And now, in your epistle you have censured me, but it mattereth not; I am not angry, but do rejoice in the greatness of your heart" (Alma 61:9). Sometimes when one of our local leaders ruffles our feathers a bit we can be like Pahoran and accept the counsel as it *should* have been given. When we are called and sustained with little fanfare and then released with even less appreciation, we can remind ourselves whose Church this really is and who it is we are actually serving. Reconciliation occurs more readily while we're counting our blessings than when auditing our grievances.

Conflict Among Family Members

Just as multi-ethnic nations can become cauldrons of conflict, so can families. The merging of moral agency within a household of parents and children is not an easy process when there are great differences in age, gender, physical strength, energy levels, intellectual agility, experience, and birth order, all providing a potential seedbed for conflict. Indeed, the Savior himself said that His coming into the world would "set a man at variance against his father, and the daughter against her mother, and the daughter in law against her mother in law. And a man's foes shall be they of his own household." (Matthew 10:35–36.) Some of the greatest acts of violence and abuse occur within the family setting, and the tragedy is compounded by the fact that important emotional attachments are often severed, attachments that should have been strengthened with the passage of time. Elder Neal A. Maxwell acknowledged that "many parents love and care but experience unreciprocated love. This is part of coming to know, on our small scale, what Jesus experienced." ("Enduring Well," *Ensign*, April, 1997, p. 8.)

Those who do not honor their parents, or parents who fail to properly love and care for their children, are not able to enjoy the rest of the Lord. Latter-day prophets have carefully taught us of the importance of family prayer, family home

evening, regular scripture study, father's blessings, and attendance at Church meetings together. Still, each individual
within the family has moral agency, and when the exercise of
that agency differs appreciably from the expectations of others,
the family members are not at rest.

Reconciliation Within the Family

The Spirit of Elijah is a real power and can be a mending,
healing influence in literally turning the hearts of the children
to their parents and the hearts of the parents to their children.
As with the Savior's gradual healing of the blind man in Bethsaida in stages (see Mark 8:22–25), a family sincerely striving
for reconciliation may bring about the healing of wounds and
the removal of scars gradually, in stages. It is extremely important that this process include both truth *and* reconciliation, for
as William Blake reminds us, "A Truth that's told with bad intent / Beats all the Lies you can invent" (William Blake, "The
Pickering Ms.: Auguries of Innocence," in John Sampson, ed.,
The Poems of William Blake [London: Senate, 1995], p. 210).

The Apostle Paul taught the Ephesians the importance of
"speaking the truth in love" (Ephesians 4:15), and Elder Russell
M. Nelson has reaffirmed that "when truth is magnified by
mercy or refined by righteousness, it can be converted from a
force that can destroy to a force that can bless" ("Truth and
More," *Ensign,* January 1986, p. 73). When a sincere desire for
righteous reconciliation is included in telling the truth, hypo-
critical and hypercritical parents will humble themselves and
ask the forgiveness of their children for unkind acts and flawed
examples of the past. Such parents can, in the words of T. S.
Eliot, acknowledge their awareness "Of things ill done and
done to others' harm which once [they] took for exercise of
virtue." And children can apologize to parents and siblings for
their self-centered, immature behavior of the past, "And the
end of all [their] exploring will be to arrive where [they] started"

(T. S. Eliot, "Little Gidding," in *Collected Poems: 1909–1962* [London: Faber and Faber, 1974], pp. 118–19) and to realize that the family is a life-long laboratory for learning how to love others despite their imperfections.

Reconciliation Between Brothers

Both the Old Testament and the Book of Mormon are replete with examples of families who faced hardships and heartbreaks. Adam and Eve faced the sorrow of Cain's nefarious actions. Lehi and Sariah suffered the rebellion of Laman and Lemuel. Alma the Elder, with the Lord's help, rescued his son, and then Alma the Younger had his own struggles with his missionary son Corianton. Ofttimes the greater need for reconciliation is not between parents and children but rather between brothers and sisters who finally declare an end to "sibil war."

There is, perhaps, no more poignant case of contention turned to conciliation than the lives of Jacob and Esau. When Isaac, the son of Abraham, was forty years old, he married Rebekah, and after she had been barren for twenty years, Isaac importuned the Lord for the blessing of children. When Isaac was sixty years old the Lord blessed Rebekah with twin sons. The first was Esau who was born "red, all over like an hairy garment." The second boy was Jacob, and "Isaac loved Esau . . . but Rebekah loved Jacob." (Genesis 25:20–28.)

Esau was an outdoorsman who loved to go hunting, in contrast to Jacob, who preferred "dwelling in tents." On one occasion Esau returned from the hunt utterly famished and asked his brother for some pottage the latter had prepared. Jacob told his brother he could have some pottage only if Esau would sell him the birthright belonging to the firstborn son. Esau replied: "Behold, I am at the point to die: and what profit shall this birthright do to me?" Jacob solemnized the transaction by requiring Esau to swear that the birthright now was Jacob's. Thus "Esau despised his birthright" (Genesis 25:30–34).

Isaac grew old and his eyes failed him. One day he called Esau to himself and asked him to go hunting and prepare some "savoury meat," with the promise of a father's blessing afterward. Rebekah overheard the conversation, and after Esau had departed for the fields she told Jacob to fetch two goat kids with which she could prepare a meal for Isaac. Jacob was very uneasy about this whole business, contending that his father would perceive him to be a deceiver and bring a curse upon him "and not a blessing." Rebekah rejoined: "Upon me be thy curse, my son: only obey my voice." She then had Jacob "put the skins of the kids of the goats upon his hands." (Genesis 27:1–16.)

As Jacob brought the meat and bread to his father, Isaac asked: "Who art thou, my son?" Jacob claimed to be "Esau thy firstborn." The elderly sightless man finally concluded: "The voice is Jacob's voice, but the hands are the hands of Esau." Yet again he asked if for certainty Esau stood before him, and Jacob replied that he was, indeed, Esau. After eating the meal, Isaac gave Jacob the birthright blessing, including the promise that nations would "bow down" to him. (Genesis 27:17–29.)

Almost immediately after the pronouncement of the blessing upon Jacob, Esau returned from hunting, only to be told by his father: "Thy brother came with subtilty, and hath taken away thy blessing." Extremely disappointed and irritated, Esau exclaimed: "He hath supplanted me these two times: he took away my birthright; and, behold, now he hath taken away my blessing" and "he lifted up his voice, and wept." The scriptures record that "Esau hated Jacob" and he secretly vowed that after his father passed away he would slay Jacob (Genesis 27:30–41.)

Isaac, having counseled Jacob not to marry any of the Canaanite young women, sent Jacob to seek a wife at his uncle Laban's place in Padanaram, and there he fell in love with his cousin Rachel. He struck an agreement with his uncle that he could marry Rachel after working for Laban for seven years, "and they seemed unto him but a few days, for the love he had to her" (Genesis 29:20). But at the end of the seven years, through intrigue and deception, Laban required him to first marry Rachel's older sister, Leah. Seven more years Jacob served Laban for Rachel. He then worked an additional six years in return for a herd of cattle. Now, after twenty years in the servitude of his father-in-law, the time had come for Jacob and his family to strike out on their own. (Genesis 31:7–41.)

As Jacob and his entourage anticipated passing through the land of Seir where Esau was known to have settled, Jacob received word that Esau was approaching with a company of men. The two brothers had not seen each other for two decades, and "Jacob was greatly afraid and distressed," at the prospect of encountering his presumably angry brother. In order to protect the lives of his family members, he divided the people and the animals into two groups, reasoning that "If Esau come to the one company, and smite it, then the other company which is left shall escape." Jacob then turned to the Lord in mighty prayer, imploring Him for protection, that his brother Esau might not harm his family. (Genesis 32:3–11.)

Jacob then prepared for Esau an extravagant present consisting of many different kinds of livestock and sent them on ahead (Genesis 32:13–18). When the moment of the tense encounter between Jacob and Esau finally arrived, Jacob "bowed himself to the ground seven times, until he came near to his brother. And Esau ran to meet him, and embraced him, and fell on his neck, and kissed him: and they wept." (Genesis 33:1–4.) Esau then asked about the presence of the numerous animals Jacob had brought with him, and Jacob told him that the large herd of animals was a conciliatory gift to him. Esau replied: "I have enough, my brother; keep that thou hast unto thyself," but after further importuning from Jacob, Esau finally agreed to accept his brother's generous gifts. Many centuries later the Apostle John would write "He that loveth his brother abideth in the light, and there is none occasion of stumbling in him" (1 John 2:10). Up to twenty years of animosity, covetousness, thoughts of vengeance, and fear of retaliation had come to an end. These twin brothers had passed through two decades of darkness into the light. They were now at rest.

Reconciliation Between Mother and Daughter

Sister Julia Campbell is a bright young woman whose talent as a poetess reflects wisdom far beyond her years. I was so taken by one of her poems that I telephoned her to ask for a little background. Fortunately, she was reared in a loving and supportive home of faithful Latter-day Saints, but she has a good friend who is far less fortunate. Her friend's plight prompted Julia to compose the following poem reflecting the spirit of reconciliation and rest within a family fraught with turmoil and strife:

Mother

If I could pull from you
The child you were,
I would rock her gently in my arms,
and hold her hand
until it stops shaking.
I would sing soporific lullabies,
leave the light on
all night,
and whisper, "I love you,"
before I close the door.
She would not sleep
in a dark corner that reeks of booze
and sweat, or wince
at every sound.
I would send her to school
in a brand-new dress
and shiny Mary-Janes,
so her classmates wouldn't snicker
or exclude her from their games

of hopscotch and tag.
She wouldn't have to wear
long-sleeved sweaters, in the summer,
to hide the bruises from home.
I would make sure
she was happy and knew love;
then I would lay her in your arms,
Mother,
and we would watch her sleep
peacefully.
(Julia Campbell, *New Era*, August, 1996, p. 22.)

Return of the Prodigal Son

Several years ago I was invited by a venerable English professor to participate in his seminar on the world's great literature. Among many other literary works, we analyzed in detail the parable of the prodigal son found in Luke chapter 15. I was slightly surprised by the inclusion of this particular parable in a seminar on great literature, for at least three reasons. First, the English department already had a course entitled "The Bible as Literature." Second, I knew the professor was an erudite man with impeccable internationally recognized credentials as a literary critic who, I assumed, would be inclined to focus upon secular rather than sacred literature. Third, I naively assumed that if a scholar in English literature were going to analyze a particular biblical passage it would more likely be poetic, Psalm 23, or perhaps the Sermon on the Mount, or Matthew 25: "For I was an hungred, and ye gave me meat: I was thirsty, and ye gave me drink: I was a stranger, and ye took me in . . . "

I gained many new insights into the various works we analyzed throughout the semester, and I shall long remember the day we sat around a large table reading the parable of the prodigal son. I thought we would dissect the work in terms of its embedded symbolism and unravel obscure metaphors, as we had done with other works. But at the conclusion of our reading the parable, the professor began to speak, and with a catch in his voice and with tear-filled eyes he confessed: "I love this parable because it is the story of my life." This respected scholar who had acquired an ample share of the accolades of men had humbled himself and accepted the restored gospel of Jesus Christ and had become reconciled with his Father in Heaven. I feel certain that he could well have echoed the words of the Prophet Joseph Smith that "no one need suppose me guilty of any great or malignant sins. A disposition to commit such was never in my nature." (Joseph Smith—History 1:28.) But through his conversion he was the first to admit that "all have sinned, and come short of the glory of God" (Romans 3:23). When he joined the Church, the "prodigal son" had returned home.

To Any Who Have Watched for a Son's Returning

He watched his son gather all the goods
that were his lot,
anxious to be gone from tending flocks,
the dullness of the fields.
He stood by the olive tree gate long
after the caravan disappeared
where the road climbs the hills
on the far side of the valley,
into infinity.
Through changing seasons he spent the light
in a great chair, facing the far country,
and that speck of road on the horizon.
Mocking friends: "He will not come."
Whispering servants: "The old man
has lost his senses."
A chiding son: "You should not have let him go."
A grieving wife: "You need rest and sleep."
She covered his drooping shoulders,

his callused knees, when east winds blew chill, until
    that day . . .
A form familiar, even at infinity,
in shreds, alone, stumbling over pebbles.
"When he was a great way off,
His father saw him,
and had compassion, and ran,
and fell on his neck, and kissed him."
        (Luke 15:20)
(Mary Lyman Henrie, *Ensign*, March 1983, p. 63.)

A Prodigal Father

On occasion, it is the righteous son who must accept the return of a prodigal father who may have been an alcoholic, or a
philanderer, or simply someone extremely resistant to religion
and insensitive to the things of the Spirit. Such was the case
with the father of one of our priesthood leaders in Europe.
When this particular leader was a young man living at home,
the missionaries taught the gospel to his family, and he, his sister, and his mother all decided to enter the waters of baptism
over the vehement protestations of the family patriarch.
Church membership became a great source of contention in
their home. The conflict between father and daughter was particularly intense.

Eventually the children left home, acquired advanced education and training, married, and established families of their
own. Whenever the married children would visit their parental
home the subject of religion was generally avoided. Then, with
the passage of time, the father of the extended family grew ill,
and it was apparent that he would probably not live much
longer. Concerned for his father's welfare, his son, now a prominent leader in the Church in his area, would regularly call his
father to offer comfort and support in his declining years. One
day this faithful son felt a prompting to write his nonmember

father a letter in which he expressed his love and gratitude for the sacrifices his father had made in his behalf and thanking him for his sterling example in so many areas of his life. His father had worked very hard, and he was a very generous man in many ways.

The son telephoned his father a few days after the letter had been sent, but his dad made no mention of the letter he had received. After a few more phone calls the son pointedly asked his father if he had not received the letter. There was a long pause, and it was obvious that his aging father was struggling to gain his composure before speaking. Finally he broke the silence: "Son, why did you wait so long to send me that letter? It would have made such a big difference if I had received it several years earlier." Choking back the tears, this son learned that for many years his father had evidently felt that his earlier recalcitrance toward the Church and his earlier criticism of his wife and children had disqualified him from claiming the blessings of the gospel in his life. He was proud of his children and their exemplary lives, and he had recognized the impact of the gospel in their lives. He had conceded to himself that they had been right and he had been wrong. All he needed was an overture of reconciliation to express his innermost desires and feelings. But pride and a history of the past often become barriers to reconciliation. Clearly, there is no better day than today to make that phone call, to write that important letter, or to take time to make that all-important visit.

A Prodigal Partner

A dear family friend, a mother in Zion who was truly without guile, recently left this earth to dwell in paradise. After she had borne several children during financially straitened times, her husband suddenly completely disappeared, leaving her with the sole responsibility for rearing their children. With extraordinary skills as a seamstress she was able to keep bread on the table and to feed her little flock until each in turn was able to contribute to the family income and then to leave the nest armed with the ability to work hard. Each child was able to become fully self-reliant and to rear a righteous family unto the Lord. During their growing up years their mother never denigrated their absentee father. There was no bitterness and no self-pity. They simply accepted the task of pushing and pulling their own handcart into the valley, as it were.

Long after all the children had left home, and a few years after this dear sister's retirement, she heard a surprise knock at the door. To her overwhelming surprise it was her husband, who had been missing for several decades. "My dear," he said with trembling lips, "I'm very sick. Will you take care of me?" "Of course I will," was her immediate reply. "Come on in. It's good to see you again."

There are many who would say her judgment was impaired and that he did not deserve such immediate acceptance. But those who would make such judgments of her do not understand the gospel, the Atonement, and the parable of the prodigal son in the way she did. She wished to be forgiven of her debts as she forgave her debtor (see Matthew 6:12; D&C 64:8–10).

Reconciliation between parents and children on earth is necessary to assure the promises of the sealing ordinances performed in the house of the Lord, and if our children are to be reconciled with their Heavenly Father we should make sure that they are also reconciled to their earthly parents and to each other. Sometimes this reconciliation requires the realization by children that their parents were doing the very best they could under the circumstances and that the parents may have also experienced a pock-marked childhood and were, themselves, still gradually healing from previous wounds of childhood and the scars of adolescence. The atonement of Jesus Christ, or at-one-ment, is efficacious in our lives when we become reconciled with Him and become at one with others.

When members of strife-ridden families eventually become at one, they begin to travel the pathway to perfection and gain a particular appreciation for the Savior's injunction: "Greater love hath no man than this, that a man lay down his life for his friends" (John 15:13). Sometimes family members financially support a brother or their parents. In some families, one member has gladly donated a kidney or bone marrow for another member of the family. Some family members literally become willing to die for one another, and, even more important, they look forward to living together for time and for all eternity.

Six

God Hath Not Ceased to Be a God of Miracles

ABOUT EIGHT DECADES BEFORE THE SAVIOR'S birth, Alma prophesied to the people in the land of Gideon that the Son of God would soon come to earth, and He would "go forth, suffering pains and afflictions and temptations of every kind; and this that the word might be fulfilled which saith he will take upon him the pains and the sicknesses of his people. And he will take upon him death, that he may loose the bands of death which bind his people; and he will take upon him their infirmities, that his bowels may be filled with mercy, according to the flesh, that he may know according to the flesh how to succor his people according to their infirmities." (Alma 7:11–12.)

As the Lord performed countless miracles and took upon himself "the pains and the sicknesses of His people," the lesson became clear: if He could heal blindness, He can also heal a broken heart. If He could heal leprosy, He can cleanse those who are spiritually unclean. If He could cast out devils, He can also lift the spirits of those who are depressed. If He could make the lame to walk, He can restore a spring to the step of those who are downtrodden.

Miracles at Cana

Throughout His earthly ministry the Savior devoted His entire time and energy to teaching and blessing others. His first recorded miracle occurred at the wedding in Cana, when He turned the water to wine (John 2:1–11). Soon afterward he was approached by a nobleman whose son was seriously ill with a high fever, and as any concerned parent would do, the nobleman implored the Savior to come to his home and heal his son. The Savior replied reassuringly: "Go thy way; thy son liveth." The nobleman believed the Savior and returned home to find that his son had recovered "at the same hour, in the which Jesus said unto him, Thy son liveth" (John 4:46–53). The Savior's recorded miracles began at Cana, but they continued throughout His earthly ministry as the prophecy unfolded that "the Lord God will wipe away tears from off all faces" (Isaiah 25:8). Regardless of the source of the sorrow and anguish, whether they be physical or psychological or emotional or spiritual in origin, the Lord God of Israel will give to the distressed "beauty for ashes, the oil of joy for mourning, the garment of praise for the spirit of heaviness" (Isaiah 61:3).

Rebuking an Unclean Spirit

While teaching in the synagogue in Capernaum the Savior was accosted by a man possessed of an unclean spirit which cried out: "Let us alone; what have we to do with thee, thou Jesus of Nazareth?" Jesus rebuked the evil spirit and commanded him to depart from the man, and the people "were all amazed" that his authority was so great that even unclean spirits obeyed him (Mark 1:21–28). It is significant that on this and other occasions unclean spirits, apparently retaining their knowledge of the pre-mortal Christ and the council and subsequent war in heaven, immediately recognized Christ as the Son of God, something that took many mortal men much longer to acknowledge. (See Luke 4:33–34; Mark 5:7–9; Matthew 8:28–34; Luke 8:26–39.)

Healing the Leper

Reports of the Savior's miracles were being spread abroad, and as He descended the mountains near Galilee he encountered a leper who besought a healing blessing, and Jesus touched him and said "Be thou clean," and he was immediately healed. Jesus then admonished him to "Say nothing to any man." However, human nature being such as it is, "he went out, and began to publish it much, and to blaze abroad the matter, insomuch that Jesus could no more openly enter into the city" (Mark 1:40–45; Matthew 8:1–4; Luke 5:12–15).

The Centurion's Servant

Returning to Capernaum Jesus was approached by a centurion whose servant was tormented with palsy. The Savior offered to come to the centurion's home, but the man gently resisted, saying, "Lord, I am not worthy that thou shouldest come under my roof: but speak the word only, and my servant shall be healed." Jesus replied: "I have not found so great faith, no, not in Israel. Go thy way; and as thou hast believed, so be it done unto thee." And his servant was immediately healed. (Matthew 8:5–13; Luke 7:1–10.)

Raising the Widow's Son from the Dead

While visiting the city of Nain, the Savior observed that "a dead man was carried out, the only son of a widow." Moved with compassion for her, Jesus touched the bier and commanded the young man to arise, and "he that was dead sat up, and began to speak." And the people "glorified God, saying, That a great prophet is risen up among us; and, that God hath visited his people" (Luke 7:11–17).

Healing Peter's Mother-in-Law

Jesus again returned to Capernaum, where He visited the mother-in-law of Peter the Apostle, who lay ill from a fever, "And He touched her hand, and the fever left her: and she arose, and ministered unto them" (Matthew 8:14–15; Mark 1:30–31; Luke 4:38–41). (Those who would contend that celibacy was a tradition among the leaders of the Church in ancient times ignore three apostolic witnesses who unmistakably recorded that Peter, the chief Apostle, was indeed married.)

Casting Evil Spirits into Gadarene Swine

Immediately after the Savior's arrival on the Gadarene coast on the opposite shore of Galilee He was approached by a man with an unclean spirit who had been dwelling among the tombs. The man was extremely tormented, and though some had tried to bind him, he invariably broke his fetters and chains. When he saw Jesus from afar he ran and worshipped Him, and cried: "What have I to do with thee, Jesus, thou Son of the most high God? I adjure thee by God, that thou torment me not." Jesus then commanded: "Come out of the man, thou unclean spirit." The Savior then asked his name, to which he replied: "My name is Legion: for we are many." On the nearby hills was a large herd of swine. The devils besought Jesus that he might permit them to enter the swine, "and forthwith Jesus gave them leave. And the unclean spirits went out, and entered into the swine: and the herd ran violently down a steep place into the sea, (they were about two thousand;) and were choked in the sea." (Mark 5:1–13.)

The Woman Touched the Hem of His Garment

A certain ruler in Capernaum by the name of Jairus approached Jesus with the report that his daughter had just died.

The grieving father petitioned the Savior to "come and lay thy hand upon her, and she shall live." Responding to the man's plea, the Savior began to follow him home, and while this was under way "a woman, which was diseased with an issue of blood twelve years, came behind him, and touched the hem of His garment: and immediately her issue of blood [ceased]." The Savior asked, "Who touched me?" Those who heard the question explained that, in the midst of a multitude of people pressing against him, it was impossible to know who touched his clothes. But Jesus persisted: "Somebody hath touched me: for I perceive that virtue is gone out of me." With trembling apprehension the woman came forward and explained why she had grabbed the hem of His garment, and Jesus compassionately said to her, "Daughter, be of good comfort; thy faith hath made thee whole." (Luke 8:43–48; Mark 5:25–34; Matthew 9:20–22.)

Jairus's Daughter Raised from the Dead

By the time the Master and His disciples had arrived at the home of Jairus, many people had gathered there. Jesus asked them to make room for Him to see the ruler's daughter, for, said He: "the maid is not dead, but sleepeth." The inquisitive onlookers "laughed him to scorn," but notwithstanding their jeers the Savior "took her by the hand, and the maid arose. And the fame hereof went abroad into all that land" (Matthew 9:23–26; Mark 5:21–24; Luke 4:40–41).

Two Blind Men

As Jesus departed from Jairus's home He was followed by two blind men who accosted him with the plea, "Thou Son of David, have mercy on us." He then asked them: "Believe ye that I am able to do this?" and they replied affirmatively: "Yea, Lord." He then touched their eyes and said, "According to your faith be it unto you," and their sight was restored. He exhorted them to keep the manner of their healing confidential "that no man know it" (Matthew 9:27–31).

Dumb Man Possessed of a Devil

While the Savior was in Capernaum the people "brought to him a dumb man possessed with a devil," and as soon as Jesus cast the devil out of the man he began to speak, to the amazement of those around him. "But the Pharisees said, He casteth out devils through the prince of devils." (Matthew 9:32–34; Luke 11:14–15.) Considerably later, when the Savior was with His disciples at Caesarea Philippi, Peter testified: "Thou art the Christ, the Son of the living God." Jesus then taught Peter the important principle that he had not received this strong testimony through "flesh and bone," or from the physical senses, but rather through "my Father which is in heaven," through a manifestation of the Spirit. (Matthew 16:13–17.) This point was entirely lost on the Pharisees, whose preconceptions and prejudices excluded the manifestations of the Spirit in their lives.

A Man with a Withered Hand

The Master spent many Sabbath days in the synagogues teaching and healing the sick, and whenever He performed miracles on the Sabbath He generally generated a good deal of criticism from the Pharisees. On one such occasion the Pharisees sought to entrap Jesus by pointing to a man with a withered hand and asking the Savior whether it was lawful to heal on the Sabbath. The Master Teacher asked those who would falsely accuse Him what one of them would do if his only sheep fell into a pit on the Sabbath. Would they not lift it out? Continuing, He asked: "How much then is a man better than a sheep? Wherefore it is lawful to do well on the sabbath days." He then told the man to stretch forth his hand. "And he stretched it forth; and it was restored whole, like as the other."

And thereafter the Pharisees counseled among themselves "how they might destroy him." (Matthew 12:9–14; Mark 3:1–6; Luke 6:6–11.)

The Lame Man at the Pool of Bethesda

In Jerusalem there was a pool of water called Bethesda, and tradition held that "an angel went down at a certain season into the pool, and troubled the water; whosoever then first after the troubling of the water stepped in was made whole of whatsoever disease he had." Thus the pool was surrounded by many who were physically afflicted and who waited for the moving of the water, at which time each would try to enter the pool first. Near the edge of the pool lay a man who had suffered an infirmity for thirty-eight years. He explained to the Savior that, because of his weakness, he was unable to reach the pool before the others, and no one seemed inclined to help him enter the pool while the waters were in motion. Filled with compassion, the Savior commanded him, "Rise, take up thy bed, and walk." But as this grateful man did so, there were detractors who thereafter sought the Savior's life "because he had done these things on the sabbath day" (John 5:2–16).

Feeding the Five Thousand

Jesus went northward and across the Sea of Galilee, where He was followed by a great multitude. Sensing their need for physical nourishment, He asked Philip, "Whence shall we buy bread, that these may eat?" Philip opined that their collective resources would not be adequate to feed such a crowd of people. Then Andrew came to the Master and said, "There is a lad here, which hath five barley loaves, and two small fishes: but what are they among so many?" But the Savior blessed these meager morsels, and the disciples distributed them to the masses of people; and when all had had their fill there were twelve baskets full of food remaining. Teaching an important welfare principle, Jesus instructed His disciples to "gather up the fragments that remain, that nothing be lost." (John 6:5–14; Matthew 14:16–21; Mark 6:33–44; Luke 9:11–17.)

The feeding of the five thousand was indeed a great miracle, as was the Savior's demonstration of the miracles that can occur in our individual lives when we bring forth to Him all we have, even if it be but five barley loaves and two fishes. The gathering of the fragments of bread remaining may also symbolize His love for every one of His Father's children and their concern that "nothing be lost," but that *all* be gathered in.

Walking on the Water

Jesus suggested to His disciples that they sail to the other side of the Sea of Galilee while he dispersed the multitudes. During "the fourth watch of the night" the disciples spotted Jesus walking toward them on the sea, and "they cried out for fear," but Jesus dispelled their anxieties, saying, "Be of good cheer; it is I; be not afraid." Peter responded: "Lord, if it be thou, bid me come unto thee on the water," and the Savior said, "Come." As Peter began walking on the water, he observed the wind-tossed waves and he became frightened and began to sink. He cried, "Lord, save me." Jesus compassionately reached down and caught him, and said, "O thou of little faith, wherefore didst thou doubt?" (Matthew 14:22–33; Mark 6:45–52; John 6:16–21.)

It was a miracle to walk on water, and here the Savior performed other miracles in Peter's life. First, he saved him from drowning. Second, he gently reproved him for his lack of faith, thereby kindling in Peter a greater desire to increase his faith. And third, he did not release Peter but retained him as His chief disciple. He did not give up on Peter because of a temporary lack of faith. A restoration of self-worth and self-confidence constitutes no small miracle.

They Laid the Sick in the Streets

As they reached the opposite shore and "came into the land of Gennesaret," those who had heard the reports of the Savior's miraculous healing power "brought unto him all that were diseased," and they "laid the sick in the streets" hoping only to be able to touch the hem of His garment and be healed, "and as many as touched [him] were made whole" (Matthew 14:34–36; Mark 6:53–56). On another occasion as Jesus came "into the coasts of Judea" "great multitudes followed him; and he healed them there" (Matthew 19:1–2).

Because the Savior is both just and merciful, the healing of the multitudes was not limited to the inhabitants of ancient Israel but was also graciously extended to the people of the Western Hemisphere during His visit to them following His resurrection. After teaching the ancient Nephites, the Savior perceived that their faith was sufficient to heal their sick, "and he did heal them every one as they were brought forth unto him . . . and they did bathe his feet with their tears." (3 Nephi 17:1–10.) The Book of Mormon provides the comforting assurance that "God has not ceased to be a God of miracles" (Mormon 9:15).

The Canaanite Woman

From Gennesaret the Savior journeyed to the regions of Tyre and Sidon. A Canaanite woman came from those regions and pleaded for a blessing for her daughter, who was "grievously vexed with a devil." He explained to her that His mission was to "the lost sheep of the house of Israel," which would have excluded her. But the woman persisted until He responded: "It is not meet to take the children's bread, and to cast it to dogs." Undaunted, she unrelentingly replied: "Truth, Lord: yet the dogs eat of the crumbs which fall from their masters' table." Sensing her great humility and her faith in Him, the Savior replied: "O woman, great is thy faith: be it unto thee even as thou wilt. And her daughter was made whole from that very hour." (Matthew 15:21–28; Mark 7:24–30.)

Healing the Lame and Feeding Four Thousand

Some time after feeding the five thousand near the shores of Galilee, the Savior went up into the mountain above the sea, and the multitudes brought "those that were lame, blind, dumb, maimed, and many others, and cast them down at Jesus' feet; and he healed them." And Jesus had compassion upon the multitude who stayed near him for three days, and he told His disciples "I will not send them away fasting, lest they faint in the way." And so, much as before, taking seven loaves and a few little fishes, He blessed them and fed "four thousand men, beside women and children" (Matthew 15:32–38; Mark 8:1–9).

Gradual Healing of Blind Man in Bethsaida

As the Savior came to Bethsaida he performed a healing like no other previously or subsequently recorded. A blind man was brought to Jesus so He could touch the man and heal him. Jesus proceeded to lead the man out of town, perhaps to gain a bit of privacy; and then He "spit on his eyes, and put his hands upon him," asking the man what he saw. The man "looked up, and said, I see men as trees, walking." In other words, he could now distinguish shadows, the darkness from the light, but his vision was not yet clear enough to discern detailed features of a human form or face. The Savior again put His hands upon the man's eyes, and this time when the man looked up he could see clearly (Mark 8:22–25). Unlike other healing miracles the Savior performed, this miracle had occurred progressively in stages. Perhaps this man, unlike others who besought the Savior with greater faith, had a hopeful *desire* that needed to be gradually strengthened into *faith*. Perhaps we could learn from this experience that a miraculous change is not always brought about during the first home teaching visit, or after the first apple pie from a visiting teacher, or after the first interview with the bishop, or even with the first set of missionary discussions. For some, the process of healing, and changing, and developing faith requires some extra visits, a few additional interviews, and more time and patience. But eventually the miracle will occur.

There are those whose trial in life is learning to live with a painful, debilitating, chronic illness, and sometimes their patience and their faith will be tried to the limit as their prayers for relief ascend heavenward without an apparent response. But the prophetic promises to the faithful will indeed be fulfilled: "the Son of Righteousness [will] arise with healing in his wings," and that which is broken will be mended, that which is missing will be restored, and that which is hurting will be healed. (See 3 Nephi 25:2; 2 Nephi 25:13; Malachi 4:2.)

Only by Prayer and Fasting

As the Savior ordained the Twelve "he gave them power against unclean spirits, to cast them out, and to heal all manner of sickness and all manner of disease" (Matthew 10:1; Mark 3:14–15). As the kingdom continued to grow He called and sent forth "other seventy" to preach the gospel (Luke 10:1–3), and when they returned to give Jesus a report of their labors they exclaimed that "even the devils are subject unto us through thy name" (Luke 10:17).

There was a singular occasion, however, when the father of a mentally disturbed son brought the young man to Jesus saying: "I brought him to thy disciples, and they could not cure him . . ." Jesus then "rebuked the devil; and he departed out of him: and the child was cured from that very hour" (Matthew 17:14–18; Mark 9:17–27). Apparently somewhat chagrined at their own inability to cast out the "foul spirit," Christ's disciples asked Him privately, "Why could not we cast him out?" Jesus forthrightly replied: "Because of your unbelief . . . If ye have faith as a grain of mustard seed, ye shall say unto this mountain, Remove hence to yonder place; and it shall remove; and nothing shall be impossible unto you. Howbeit this kind goeth not out but by *prayer and fasting.*" (Matthew 17:19–21; Mark 9:28–29; emphasis added.)

Not unlike the blind man from Bethsaida who perhaps was healed in stages as his faith increased, sometimes the faith of the healer must be incrementally increased before the miracle occurs. When the hem of His garment was touched by the woman seeking to be healed, the Savior indicated that He felt virtue leave him. It would be well for those who bestow priesthood blessings to ensure that they have an adequate supply of virtue, if you please. Patience is also an important part of faith, and in our fast-food, one-hour dry-cleaning society of instant everything we sometimes overlook the absolute importance of patience in the Lord's plan of happiness.

To the extent that it is possible to do so, the person in need of a priesthood blessing should also fast in order to claim the Lord's promised blessing that fasting can "loose the bands of wickedness" and "undo the heavy burdens," and "let the oppressed go free," and can "break every yoke" (Isaiah 58:6).

Woman with Infirmity Eighteen Years

On the Sabbath day, probably in a village of Perea, the Savior was teaching in one of the synagogues when He saw a woman "which had a spirit of infirmity eighteen years, and was bowed together, and could in no wise lift up herself." Jesus said to her: "Woman, thou art loosed from thine infirmity," and after He had laid His hands upon her she immediately "was made straight, and glorified God." As so often was the case, Jesus was criticized by the ruler of the synagogue for healing on the Sabbath. Jesus answered him sharply: "Thou hypocrite, doth not each one of you on the sabbath loose his ox or his ass from the stall, and lead him away to watering?" Pursuing this reasoning, He then asked if it would also not be appropriate for this woman to "be loosed from this bond on the sabbath day?" "And when he had said these things, all his adversaries were ashamed." (Luke 13:10–17.)

Where Are the Nine?

On His way to Jerusalem, as Jesus passed through Samaria and Galilee, He came to a village where He was met by "ten men that were lepers" who, according to the custom of the day, called from afar off that others might be warned of their contagious condition. This time, however, it was a loud voice of pleading: "Jesus, Master, have mercy on us." As the Savior viewed their pitiful plight He commanded them to show themselves "unto the priests," and "as they went, they were cleansed." "And one of them, when he saw that he was healed, turned back, and with a loud voice glorified God, and fell down on his face at his feet, giving him thanks: and he was a Samaritan." Jesus then asked him: "Were there not ten cleansed? But where are the nine? . . . Arise, go thy way: thy faith hath made thee whole." (Luke 17:11–19.) Of this event Elder Merrill J. Bateman shared the profound and poignant observation: "That day nine lepers were healed skin deep, but only one had the faith to be made whole" (Merrill J. Bateman, "The Power to Heal from Within," *Ensign*, May 1995, p. 14).

The Lord revealed that "in nothing doth man offend God, or against none is his wrath kindled, save those who confess not his hand in all things, and obey not his commandments" (D&C 59:21). President Thomas S. Monson's counsel to adopt "an attitude of gratitude" is not just sage advice but is actually a commandment of the Lord. (Thomas S. Monson, "An Attitude of Gratitude," *Ensign*, May 1992, p. 60.)

Man Born Blind at Birth

In Jerusalem on another Sabbath day Jesus encountered a man who had been born blind. This caused His disciples to ask: "Master, who did sin, this man, or his parents, that he was born blind?" The Savior responded: "Neither hath this man sinned, nor his parents: but that the works of God should be made manifest in him . . ." He then "spat on the ground, and made clay of the spittle, and he anointed the eyes of the blind man with the clay, and said unto him, Go, wash in the pool of Siloam." The blind man obeyed the Lord's command, washed the clay from his eyes, and gained his sight. Again some of the Pharisees criticized the Savior, contending, "This man is not of God, because he keepeth not the sabbath day." They then called before them the man who was healed and declared, "We know that this man is a sinner," to which the man responded: "Whether he be a sinner or no, I know not: one thing I know, that, whereas I was blind, now I see" (John 9:1–25.)

Healing of Bartimaeus

While leaving Jericho one day the Savior saw another blind man, this time a beggar by the name of Bartimaeus, sitting by the highway. When he heard that Jesus of Nazareth was passing by he cried out: "Jesus, thou Son of David, have mercy on me." Perhaps testing his faith, the Savior asked, "What wilt thou that I should do unto thee?" and Bartimaeus implored Him that he might receive his sight. "Go thy way," said Jesus, "thy faith hath made thee whole." His request was granted, and he "followed Jesus in the way." (Mark 10:46–52.)

He That Was Dead Came Forth

In the town of Bethany, not far from Jerusalem, Lazarus, the brother of Mary and Martha, became very ill, and his sisters sent an urgent request to their good friend, Jesus, to come and heal their brother. Upon receiving their request the Savior said, "This sickness is not unto death, but for the glory of God, that the Son of God might be glorified thereby." Notwithstanding the urgency of Mary and Martha's message, Jesus waited two more days before departing for Bethany. When He finally arrived, Lazarus had already been dead and in the tomb for four days. Martha exclaimed: "Lord, if thou hadst been here, my brother had not died. But I know, that even now, whatsoever thou wilt ask of God, God will give it thee." Jesus gave her the comforting assurance: "Thy brother shall rise again. . . . I am the resurrection, and the life: he that believeth in me, though he were dead, yet shall he live: and whosoever liveth and believeth in me shall never die. Believest thou this?" Demonstrating her great faith, Martha declared unequivocally: "Yea, Lord: I believe that thou art the Christ, the Son of God, which should come into the world."

Mary then approached Jesus, and when He saw her weeping for sorrow, Jesus wept, and asked the sisters: "Where have ye laid him?" As He approached the cave in which Lazarus' body lay, He commanded that the stone over the entrance be removed. He then raised his eyes heavenward and prayed: "Father, I thank thee that thou hast heard me. And I knew that thou hearest me always: but because of the people which stand by I said it, that they may believe that thou hast sent me." At the conclusion of his prayer, Jesus "cried with a loud voice, 'Lazarus, come forth.' And he that was dead came forth." (John 11:1–44).

In consequence of this mighty miracle and other miracles the Savior had performed previously "many of the Jews which came to Mary, and had seen the things which Jesus did, believed on him" (John 11:45). But there were others, blind and insensitive to the things of the Spirit, who "from that day forth . . . took counsel together for to put him to death" (John 11:53).

Many of the Pharisees and Sadducees had seen with their

own eyes miracles that Jesus had performed, but because their hearts were not pure they were blinded and unable to perceive the power by which the miracles were performed. In the words of Paul, "the natural man receiveth not the things of the Spirit of God: for they are foolishness unto him: neither can he know them, because they are spiritually discerned" (1 Corinthians 2:14). Some of the greatest miracles the Savior continues to perform are not readily discernible to the eye, for they "passeth human understanding." These miracles include unexplainable comfort in a time of distress, joy during a time of sorrow, and release from pain in the midst of anguish.

If the Savior can heal the blind, why should we find it difficult to believe He can heal us of our shyness or lack of courage in approaching others about the gospel? If Jesus could raise Lazarus from the dead, surely He can raise our spirits and remove feelings of anguish and despair. If Christ created the world in which we live, certainly He can help us create a new physical and social and spiritual environment if we will but trust in Him. If the Lord could cast out evil spirits, certainly He can also free us from our addictions and our fears.

He who created the world, He who raised Jairus's daughter, the widow's son, and Lazarus from the dead extends the comforting invitation to us all: "Come unto me, all ye that labour and are heavy laden, and I will give you rest. Take my yoke upon you, and learn of me; for I am meek and lowly in heart: and ye shall find rest unto your souls. For my yoke is easy, and my burden is light." (Matthew 11:28–30.)

The Son Can Do Nothing of Himself

Notwithstanding the countless miracles the Savior graciously performed throughout His earthly ministry, He repeatedly acknowledged that "The Son can do nothing of himself, but what he seeth the Father do" (John 5:19; see also: 5:30; 7:28; 8:28–29). In the Book of Mormon the Lord God twice declares, "I am able to do mine own work" (2 Nephi 27:20–21), but in order that others may become like Him, the Lord has shared His power and endowed His children with various spiritual gifts, including the gift of working "mighty miracles" (Moroni 10:12; D&C 46:21; 1 Corinthians 12:10). The God of comfort, the God of miracles, though He is able to do His own work, benevolently permits others to accomplish countless acts of comfort and to perform miracles in His name so that we, His children, might become more like Him.

Elder Kenneth Johnson recalled his first recollection at age five of his father returning home at the end of World War II. Although his loving mother had fostered memories of his father during his lengthy absence, young Kenneth was delighted to finally have a real live father around the house. In order to build rapport with his young son, Brother Johnson's father invited Kenneth to assist him in a variety of household do-it-yourself projects. Said Elder Johnson: "Just to be in his presence was a thrill for me. He invited me to help him by passing a hammer, a screwdriver, or some other tool. I was convinced that my help was necessary and that without me he would not be able to complete his task." (Kenneth Johnson, "We All Have a Father in Whom We Can Trust," *Ensign*, May 1994, p. 29.)

Elder Johnson likened his relationship to his earthly father to our relationship with our Heavenly Father, who provides us with countless opportunities to assist Him in performing His sacred work, even though He is able to do His own work in bringing to pass "the immortality and eternal life of man" (Moses 1:39). As He permits us to assist in His work, as we comfort and serve others and participate in priesthood ordinances and blessings, a miracle occurs, for "God has provided a means that man, through faith, might work mighty miracles; therefore he becometh a great benefit to his fellow beings." (Mosiah 8:18.)

PART TWO
God of Love

And it came to pass that I saw the heavens open;
and an angel came down and stood before me;
and he said unto me: Nephi, what beholdest thou?

And I said unto him: A virgin,
most beautiful and fair above all other virgins.

And he said unto me:
Knowest thou the condescension of God?

And I said unto him: I know that he loveth his children;
nevertheless, I do not know the meaning of all things.

And he said unto me: Behold, the virgin whom thou seest is the
mother of the Son of God, after the manner of the flesh.

And it came to pass that I beheld that she was carried away in the
Spirit; and after she had been carried away in the Spirit for the
space of a time the angel spake unto me, saying: Look!

And I looked and beheld the virgin again,
bearing a child in her arms.

And the angel said unto me: Behold the Lamb of God,
yea, even the Son of the Eternal Father!

—1 NEPHI 11:14–21

SEVEN

God So Loved
the World

ON ONE OCCASION, THE FRIENDS OF A MAN afflicted with palsy sought a blessing from the Savior while He was inside of a house speaking to a host of other people. The entrance to the house was apparently blocked by the throng of people, so it was impossible for the men to bring their bed-ridden friend through the door to request a blessing. Undaunted by this challenge, these innovative friends lifted the man's bed atop the house "and let him down through the tiling with his couch into the midst before Jesus" (Luke 5:19). When the Savior observed their persistence and their faith He turned to the man on the bed and said: "Man, thy sins are forgiven thee."

This statement caused the scribes and Pharisees who heard the Savior's declaration to ask one another, "Who is this which speaketh blasphemies? Who can forgive sins, but God alone? But when Jesus perceived their thoughts, he answering said unto them, What reason ye in your hearts? Whether is easier, to say, Thy sins be forgiven thee; or to say, Rise up and walk?" (Luke 5:20–23). Joseph Smith's inspired translation of this same passage is rendered as follows: "Does it require more power to forgive sins than to make the sick rise up and walk?" (JST Luke

5:23). To this question, Elder Bruce R. McConkie contends "there could be only one answer! They are as one; he that can do the one, can do the other." (*Doctrinal New Testament Commentary,* 3 vols. [Salt Lake City: Bookcraft, 1992], vol. 1, p. 178.)

To mortal men devoid of an understanding of the atoning sacrifice of the Son of God the response to this profound question would most likely be that healing the sick requires greater effort and power than merely to declare that one's sins have been forgiven. Notwithstanding our own inadequate comprehension of the Atonement, the Savior himself provides us with a glimpse of the agonizing anguish He personally invested in this infinite act:

> For behold, I, God, have suffered these things for all, that they might not suffer if they would repent;
> But if they would not repent they must suffer even as I;
> Which suffering caused myself, even God, the greatest of all, to tremble because of pain, and to bleed at every pore, and to suffer both body and spirit—and would that I might not drink the bitter cup, and shrink—
> Nevertheless, glory be to the Father, and I partook and finished my preparations unto the children of men. (D&C 19:16–19.)

As the Savior suffered for our sins in the Garden of Gethsemane "being in an agony he prayed more earnestly: and his sweat was as it were great drops of blood falling down to the ground" (Luke 22:44). Several biblical translations in various languages have interpreted the expression "as it were" in this passage to indicate that the Savior did not actually shed any blood at all in the garden, but that His sweat was *like* drops of blood. Thanks to modern revelation, the Savior himself has laid to rest all speculation regarding the degree of his agony in bleeding from every pore while taking upon himself the sins of the world. He has described the intensity of his suffering, which did, indeed, cause him "to bleed at every pore."

A God of Power

The Pharisees could not appreciate the profundity of the Savior's question: "Does it require more power to forgive sins than to make the sick rise up and walk?" (JST Luke 5:23.) In the due course of time, however, perhaps some of them would recognize that the power involved in forgiving sins was so incomprehensibly great that when the Savior's atonement began in the Garden of Gethsemane and continued to Golgotha, where He finally "yielded up the ghost" (Matthew 27:50), the earth began to quake (Matthew 27:54), and "the veil of the temple was rent in twain," (Mark 15:38) causing the Roman centurion to declare, "Truly this man was the Son of God" (Mark 15:39; Matthew 27:54).

Half a world away the Savior's atonement was marked on the Western Hemisphere by "a great and terrible tempest; and there was terrible thunder," followed by "great and terrible destruction" as "the highways were broken up," and "many great and notable cities were sunk, and many were burned, and many were shaken till the buildings thereof had fallen to the earth. . . . And thus the face of the whole earth became deformed," and all of this commotion lasted for "about the space of three hours," and "there were some who were carried away in the whirlwind." (3 Nephi 8:5–19.) These cataclysmic events were followed by three days of "thick darkness upon all the face of the land," and so dense was the blackened atmosphere that they could even "feel the vapor of darkness," which prevented them from kindling a fire (3 Nephi 8:20–23).

The atonement of the Son of God, even He who had created the earth under the direction of his Father, caused both the Creator and the earth He created to tremble from pain, causing "the kings of the isles of the sea" to exclaim, "The God of nature suffers" (1 Nephi 19:10–12). He who had the power to create the earth for a probationary state surely has the power to forgive the sins of those who, on occasion, fail the probationary test. Jacob asked the profound question: "If God being able to speak and the world was, and to speak and man was created, O then, why not able to command the earth, or the workmanship of his hands upon the face of it, according to his will and pleasure?" (Jacob 4:9.) Christ could readily forgive the sins of others because he had paid for those sins. Indeed, we have all quite literally been "bought with a price" (I Corinthians 6:19–20), and that price is not measured in the coin of the realm but in precious drops of divine blood.

Changing Wine to Water

The first recorded miracle occurred at the wedding in Cana when the Savior changed the water to wine, but a much more significant and lasting miracle is performed each time He changes wine back to water in the lives of those who come forth with broken hearts and contrite spirits and are blessed by the miracle of forgiveness. Throughout the scriptures we associate miracles with the Savior's raising of the dead, the healing of the lame, the deaf, the blind, the lepers, and those possessed of evil spirits, but even those raised from the dead eventually suffered physical death again. An even more important and potentially more permanent healing miracle occurred whenever the Savior pronounced those comforting words, "Thy sins are forgiven thee." The burden of a painful, crippling disease is hard to bear, but in many respects the burden of sin can produce even greater pain as physical suffering is compounded by the anguish of the soul. This anguish of body and spirit can also be removed by the touch of the Master's hand as wine is changed to water.

The Touch of the Master's Hand

'Twas battered and scarred, and the auctioneer
Thought it scarcely worth his while
To waste much time on the old violin,

But held it up with a smile:
"What am I bidden, good folks," he cried,
"Who'll start the bidding for me?"
"A dollar, a dollar"; then, "Two!" "Only two?
Two dollars, and who'll make it three?
Three dollars, once; three dollars, twice;
Going for three—" But no,
From the room, far back, a gray-haired man
Came forward and picked up the bow;
Then, wiping the dust from the old violin,
And tightening the loose strings,
He played a melody pure and sweet
As a caroling angel sings.

The music ceased, and the auctioneer,
With a voice that was quiet and low,
Said: "What am I bid for the old violin?"
And he held it up with the bow.
"A thousand dollars, and who'll make it two?
Two thousand! And who'll make it three?
Three thousand, once, three thousand, twice,
And going, and gone," said he.
The people cheered, but some of them cried,
"We do not quite understand
What changed its worth." Swift came the reply:
"The touch of a master's hand."

And many a man with life out of tune,
And battered and scarred with sin,
Is auctioned cheap to the thoughtless crowd,
Much like the old violin.
A "mess of pottage," a glass of wine;
A game—and he travels on.
He is "going" once, and "going" twice,
He's "going" and almost "gone."

But the Master comes, and the foolish crowd
Never can quite understand
The worth of a soul and the change that's wrought
By the touch of the Master's hand.

(Myra Books Welch, in *The Best Loved Poems of the American People*, selected by Hazel Felleman [New York: Doubleday, 1936], pp. 222–23.)

She Washed His Feet with Tears

A Pharisee named Simon invited the Savior to come to his house. As they were eating a meal together, an uninvited woman who was known to be a sinner came into the house, approached Jesus, and "began to wash his feet with tears, and did wipe them with the hairs of her head, and kissed his feet, and anointed them with the ointment" which she had brought in an alabaster box. As Simon observed the woman's behavior and the Savior's not sending her away, the Pharisee was perplexed, and said to himself, "This man, if he were a prophet, would have known who and what manner of woman this is that toucheth him: for she is a sinner."

The Savior, discerning Simon's thoughts, shared with him an insightful parable: "There was a certain creditor which had two debtors: the one owed five hundred pence, and the other fifty. And when they had nothing to pay, he frankly forgave them both. Tell me therefore, which of them will love him most?"

"Simon answered and said, 'I suppose that he, to whom he forgave most.' And he said unto him, 'Thou hast rightly judged.'" The Master then said to Simon: "I entered into thine house, thou gavest me no water for my feet: but she hath washed my feet with tears, and wiped them with the hairs of her head. Thou gavest me no kiss: but this woman since the time I came in hath not ceased to kiss my feet. My head with oil thou didst not anoint: but this woman hath anointed my feet with ointment. Wherefore I say unto thee, Her sins, which are many, are forgiven; for she loved much: but to whom little is forgiven, the same loveth little."

"And they that sat at meat with him began to say within themselves, 'Who is this that forgiveth sins also?' And he said to the woman, 'Thy faith hath saved thee; go in peace' " (Luke 7:36–50).

In my humble judgment the account of this miracle, the miracle of forgiveness, is as tender and moving and profound as any of the Savior's other recorded miracles in which the physically and mentally afflicted were healed.

After the Savior's crucifixion the ancient inhabitants of the Western Hemisphere witnessed great destruction, as had been prophesied by Samuel the Lamanite prophet four decades previously (Helaman 14:20–29). As the survivors of the great earthquakes and floods were enveloped by impenetrable darkness, they heard the Savior's voice from the heavens: "O all ye that are spared because ye were more righteous than they, will ye not now return unto me, and repent of your sins, and be converted, that I may heal you?" (3 Nephi 9:13.)

I wholeheartedly concur with Moroni that "God has not ceased to be a God of miracles" (Mormon 9:15), and that miracles continue to happen each time a sin-sick soul enters the waters of baptism, each time troubled teenagers unload their problems on a loving bishop, and each time a struggling yet worthy person enters the precincts of a holy temple. The temple is not just a place of sealing but also a place of healing, a house of miracles, a house of God.

The Prophet Joseph Smith declared that "all sin, and all blasphemies, and every transgression, except one, that man can be guilty of, may be forgiven; and there is a salvation for all men, either in this world or the world to come, who have not committed the unpardonable sin, there being a provision either in this world or the world of spirits" (*Teachings of the Prophet*

Joseph Smith, pp. 356–57). Another servant of the Lord, President Boyd K. Packer, provides a second witness that, with the exception of the sons of perdition, "there is no habit, no addiction, no rebellion, no transgression, no apostasy, no crime exempted from the promise of complete forgiveness. That is the promise of the atonement of Christ." (Boyd K. Packer, "The Brilliant Morning of Forgiveness," *Ensign*, November 1995, p. 20.) We must pay the consequences of our sins, and that price requires a broken heart and a contrite spirit and may even include the temporary loss of certain privileges of Church membership and the suspension of temple blessings, but as the Lord assured Alma, those who confess their sins and repent of them shall be forgiven, and "as often as my people repent will I forgive them their trespasses against me" (Mosiah 26:29–30).

A living prophet, President Gordon B. Hinckley, assured the youth of Zion: "Don't ever feel that you can't be forgiven. Our Father in Heaven loves you. He is your Father. He is your Heavenly Parent. He has great concern for you. He reaches out to you in love and in forgiveness. . . . The Lord has said, 'I the Lord will forgive whom I will forgive, but of you it is required to forgive all men' (D&C 64:10). That is a mandate to us. Our Father in Heaven will take care of the forgiveness. You put it behind you. You talk with your bishop. You live in righteousness. You do what is right and things will work out for you." (*Teachings of Gordon B. Hinckley* [Salt Lake City: Deseret Book, 1997], p. 231.) All can be comforted and everyone can be healed. Of particular interest to the youth is the Lord's assurance that "they who have sought me early shall find rest to their souls" (D&C 54:10).

God So Loved the World

As the hour arrived when the Savior of the world began to atone for our sins, he uttered a great prayer of intercession in behalf of all of his Heavenly Father's children, saying: "And this is life eternal, that they might know thee the only true God, and Jesus Christ, whom thou hast sent" (John 17:3). Unfortunately, many of the earth's inhabitants know neither Christ nor His Father, and some readers of the Bible superficially describe Jehovah of the Old Testament as a God of vengeance while Jesus Christ of the New Testament is viewed as a God of mercy. (For a recent example of such thinking see: John Kennedy, "Christians should beware the terrors of the Bible," *The Guardian*, Manchester, England, February 22, 1997; Rabbi Shmuel Boteach, "Murder and mayhem? Just don't take the Bible literally," *The Guardian*, March 1, 1997.)

God's mercy is abundantly clear in Jesus' declaration to Nicodemus: "God so loved the world, that he gave his only begotten Son, that whosoever believeth in him should not perish, but have everlasting life. For God sent not his Son into the world to condemn the world; but that the world through him might be saved." (John 3:16–17.) Jesus Christ is our advocate with the Father, and because He died for our sins His advocacy is that of one who paid the price in divine drops of blood, "Wherefore, Father," he pleads, "spare these my brethren that believe on my name, that they may come unto me and have everlasting life." (D&C 45:3–5.)

Jesus Christ Is Jehovah

Following His resurrection the Savior visited the ancient Nephites and found that some of them did not understand His teachings regarding the law of Moses, "for they understood not the saying that old things had passed away, and that all things had become new." The Savior then identified himself as Jehovah, the giver of the Law, saying: "Behold, I am he that gave the law, and I am he who covenanted with my people Israel; therefore, the law in me is fulfilled, for I have come to fulfil the law; therefore it hath an end." (3 Nephi 15:2, 5.)

This was not the first time the Savior revealed His true

identity as Jehovah of the Old Testament. In the New Testament we read of His encounter with the scribes and Pharisees who claimed to be the children of Abraham, to which Jesus replied: "If ye were Abraham's children, ye would do the works of Abraham" (John 8:33–39). The Pharisees then posed the provocative question: "Art thou greater than our father Abraham, which is dead?" The Savior assertively responded: "Verily, verily, I say unto you, Before Abraham was, I am," which, in the Greek is to say, "I am Jehovah" (John 8:57–58; footnote 58b; see also Exodus 3:14). At this declaration His listeners considered His testimony to be blasphemous, "then took they up stones to cast at him" but He passed through the midst of them (John 8:59).

As the brother of Jared approached the Lord in mighty supplication to touch the sixteen transparent stones, that his people might have light in their barges, his great faith pierced the veil and he beheld Jehovah, who said to him: "Behold, this body, which ye now behold, is the body of my spirit; . . . and even as I appear unto thee to be in the spirit will I appear unto my people in the flesh" (Ether 3:16). In latter-day revelation Jesus Christ reaffirmed that He is "the Great I Am, Alpha and Omega, the beginning and the end, the same which looked upon the wide expanse of eternity, and all the seraphic hosts of heaven, before the world was made" (D&C 38:1).

On several other occasions the Savior has testified: "I am Alpha and Omega, the beginning and the ending, saith the Lord, which is, and which was, and which is to come, the Almighty" (Revelation 1:8; see also 21:6; 22:13; 3 Nephi 9:18; D&C 19:1; 45:7). He alluded to the fact that He was in the premortal council in heaven, and it was He who volunteered to fulfill the plan of the Father (see Moses 4:1–2), and it was He who created the earth under the direction of His Father (see Moses 2:1), and it was He who became the Redeemer of the world (D&C 19:1). He is Alpha and Omega, the God of the Old Testament and the God of the New Testament. He is the

God of mercy and justice, the God of compassion and accountability, but He came not "into the world to condemn the world;
but that the world through him might be saved" (John 3:17).
He is a God of comfort and a God of love.

The Apostle Paul preached that "the law [of Moses] was our
schoolmaster to bring us unto Christ" (Galatians 3:24), and
now that Christ had come to earth the law had fulfilled its purpose, and the Savior introduced a higher law reflected in his
magnificent Sermon on the Mount (Matthew 5–7; 3 Nephi
12–14). The Ten Commandments addressed behaviors, while
the Savior's higher law addressed dispositions to do evil. The
higher law required one not only to refrain from murder and
adultery and profanity but to refrain from anger, from lust, and
from swearing at all. The Savior's true disciples are to turn the
other cheek and to walk the extra mile. The higher law also
included the commandment to "love your enemies, bless them
that curse you, do good to them that hate you, and pray for
them who despitefully use you and persecute you," with the
culminating challenge: "Therefore I would that ye should be
perfect, even as I, or your Father who is in heaven is perfect"
(3 Nephi 12:48). The Book of Mormon is another testament of
Jesus Christ providing the confirmation that Jehovah of the
Old Testament is the premortal Jesus Christ (see Mosiah 13:28;
15:1; 3 Nephi 15; Ether 3:13–16).

The Savior commanded the Nephite scribes to record His
teachings regarding the gathering of His Father's children, re-
vealing that the Gentiles "may be brought to a knowledge of
me, their Redeemer, And then will I gather them in from the
four quarters of the earth; and then will I fulfil the covenant
which the Father hath made unto all the people of the house of
Israel. . . . And then will I remember my covenant which I have
made unto my people, O house of Israel, and I will bring my
gospel unto them. . . . But if the Gentiles will repent and return
unto me, saith the Father, behold they shall be numbered
among my people, O house of Israel" (3 Nephi 16:4–5, 11, 13).

These are the words of a merciful, kind and loving Son whose entire life and ministry reflected the will of His Father, the perpetual desire that every one of His children return to him.

The Prophet Joseph Smith observed that when the attribute of mercy "is once established in the mind it gives life and energy to the spirits of the saints, believing that the mercy of God will be poured out upon them in the midst of their afflictions, and that he will [be] compassionate [to] them in their sufferings, and that the mercy of God will lay hold of them and secure them in the arms of his love, so that they will receive a full reward for all their suffering" (*Lectures on Faith* 4:15). When we believe we were created in the image of a merciful God we are more likely to be optimistic, hopeful, tolerant, kind, and caring.

That wily Lucifer would have us believe that because God is merciful it is possible for mercy to rob justice and that we should ignore Nephi's warning that "there shall also be many which shall say: Eat, drink, and be merry; nevertheless, fear God—he will justify in committing a little sin . . . and if it so be that we are guilty, God will beat us with a few stripes, and at last we shall be saved in the kingdom of God" (2 Nephi 28:8). Justice requires accountability for our actions and the acceptance of the consequences of our decisions. God is, indeed, merciful, but Alma poignantly reminded his wayward son Corianton that "justice exerciseth all his demands, and also mercy claimeth all which is her own; and thus, none but the truly penitent are saved. What, do ye suppose that mercy can rob justice? I say unto you, Nay; not one whit. If so, God would cease to be God." (Alma 42:24–25.)

Satan would also seek to distort the law of justice into becoming a tool of never-ending discouragement, hopelessness, and despair. If we perceive the heavens to be governed by a God of vengeance, we are more likely to be pessimistic, judgmental, intolerant, and unkind. But there is a gentle side to justice. When those who face countless trials during their earthly probation endure faithfully to the end, they will receive their just compensation in the eternities to come. Because of justice, those who have been mistreated by others, or who have lived in abject poverty and extreme deprivation, or have experienced war, misery, and strife, will be fully compensated for the lack of joy and security they experienced in mortality. The Lord will judge the poor and the meek with righteousness and with equity (2 Nephi 21:4; Isaiah 11:4), and "the Lord God will wipe away tears from off all faces" (Isaiah 25:8). Equity is a vital ingredient of justice, and Alma reminds us of how great the "inequality of man is because of sin and transgression" (Alma 28:13). To all of us who have sinned, Abinadi assures us that when we truly repent of our sins the Savior stands betwixt us and the demands of justice, He having "satisfied the demands of justice" (Mosiah 15:9).

Merciful Mid-course Corrections

The destruction of large populations of people throughout the history of the world does not constitute prima facie evidence of either rough justice or vengeance. After commanding Nephi to slay the wicked and recalcitrant Laban, the Lord told Nephi: "It is better that one man should perish than that a nation should dwindle and perish in unbelief" (1 Nephi 4:13). At no time in the earth's history, and nowhere in holy writ, can one find a single instance of God's justice being executed without having been preceded by multiple warnings by prophets on earth. The long-suffering of Deity is underscored by the fact that, in most instances, the warnings are repeated many times and precede the consequences by several years, decades, or even centuries.

There are occasions when the spiritual survival of the human race requires some merciful mid-course corrections for certain individuals and groups. Sometimes a diseased organ must be removed in order to save a person's life, and occasionally a disruptive member of society must be removed in order to protect the integrity and security of the whole society. Alma explained to Korihor the anti-Christ that "it is better that thy soul should be lost than that thou shouldst be the means of bringing many souls down to destruction" (Alma 30:47). The cleansing of the earth by the Flood, the destruction of Sodom and Gomorrah, the slaying of the three thousand worshippers of the golden calf, and the extermination of the Amalekites may well be seen in an eternal, cosmic perspective as merciful acts that prevented masses of depraved people from falling ever deeper into the depths of depravity, thus increasing their condemnation. (See Genesis 6:11–22; 7; 18:20–33; 19:1–29; Exodus 32:15–28; 1 Samuel 15:1–23.)

Shortly before physically appearing to the ancient inhabitants of the Americas, Christ spoke from the heavens to the survivors of the great holocaust that had occurred in the Western Hemisphere signifying His crucifixion and death, as prophesied previously by Samuel the Lamanite prophet (3 Nephi 9:1–2; Helaman 14:20–25). As those who were spared heard His voice, the Savior recounted the destruction of the cities of Zarahemla, Jacobugath, Laman, Josh, Gad, and Kishkumen, which had been completely destroyed by fire. The cities of Moronihah, Gadiomnah, Jacob, Gilgal, and Gimgimno had been destroyed by earthquakes or were otherwise buried with earth, and the cities of Onihah, Mocum, and Jerusalem were destroyed by floods, while the city of Moroni was sunk into the sea (3 Nephi 9:2–12). Three times the Lord clearly declared why the inhabitants of these cities had been destroyed: "that their wickedness and abominations might be hid from before my face, that the blood of the prophets and the saints whom I sent among them might not cry unto me from the ground against them." (See 3 Nephi 9:7, 9, 11.) What seems like an act of vengeance to mortal women and men can, in reality, be an act of mercy when viewed in the context of eternity. "For my thoughts are not your thoughts, neither are your ways my ways, saith the Lord. For as the heavens are higher than the earth, so are my ways higher than your ways, and my thoughts than your thoughts." (Isaiah 55:8–9.) Elder Robert L. Simpson explained that "a basic cornerstone of true justice is compassion" (Robert L. Simpson, "Courts of Love," *Ensign*, July 1972, p. 49).

The survivors of those cataclysmic events in ancient America were admonished to repent of their sins and become converted so that the Savior might heal them. He then extended His loving arm of mercy saying, "blessed are those who come unto me." He testified that He was Jesus Christ, the Son of God, the Creator of heaven and earth, that He and the Father are one, and that through His redemption the law of Moses was fulfilled. (3 Nephi 9:13–17.)

Life on earth is a period of mortal probation. For some this period is very brief and for others it is measured in several decades; but regardless of one's longevity "there was a time granted unto man to repent, yea, a probationary time, a time to repent and serve God" (Alma 42:4). Elder Russell M. Nelson, Apostle and former thoracic surgeon, has spoken of the importance of time in the process of healing: " 'As a physician analyzes a patient's problem,' he says, 'one crucial question needs an answer: Is the patient's condition one that will improve with the passage of time, or will it become worse? For example, a fractured rib will heal with only minimal care: but a deteriorating heart valve cannot heal, and with time will only worsen. The doctor's function is to convert the process from one that will not heal to one that will heal with the passage of time.' " (Lane Johnson, "Russell M. Nelson: A Study in Obedience," *Ensign*, August, 1982, p. 20.)

The Lord's actions at the time of Noah, and the destruction of the inhabitants of other wicked cities, nations, and individuals during the earth's history, can perhaps be seen as invasive, spiritual surgery removing diseased elements from the earth in order that those who came later would have the benefit of a healthier social and spiritual environment in which to experience their probationary status. Assuming the residents of

Sodom and Gomorrah got a fair start at the outset, is it not both just and merciful to let subsequent generations begin with a fresher slate? There will always be "an opposition in all things" (2 Nephi 2:11), so there should be little concern that subsequent generations are given an unfair handicap. The individual and collective sins of those destroyed in the Flood or in Sodom and Gomorrah must have indeed been reprehensible, for, generally speaking, the Lord's promise holds true for all mankind: "I, the Lord, forgive sins, and am merciful unto those who confess their sins with humble hearts" (D&C 61:2); "though your sins be as scarlet, they shall become as white as snow" (Isaiah 1:18).

It is significant to remember that eight *righteous* souls *were* spared at the time of the Flood (1 Peter 3:20). It is also well to recall that Abraham importuned the Lord not to destroy Sodom and Gomorrah if there were fifty righteous within the city, and the Lord agreed (see Genesis 18:24–26). But Abraham could not even find forty persons, nor thirty, nor twenty, nor even ten individuals who were righteous (Genesis 18:23–33). As we observe throughout the scriptures, exercising both justice and mercy the Lord never holds a close-out sale without extensive preliminary advertising by his prophets on earth. Destruction never comes as a surprise to those who observe the warning signs.

The Slippery Slope into Bondage

At least destruction has a terminal point, but another circumstance, that of falling into bondage, can be a seemingly endless condition. Whether one is in bondage to personal addictions, economic indebtedness, or political oppression, incursions upon one's moral agency are generally met with feelings of hopelessness and despair. Slipping into bondage is often a self-initiated process that occurs just as Nephi described it. Satan begins to "rage in the hearts of the children of men, and stir them up to anger against that which is good. And others will he pacify, and lull them away into carnal security. . . . and thus the devil cheateth their souls, and leadeth them carefully down to hell." (2 Nephi 28:20–21.)

In the beginning history of the human family, Satan successfully seduced Cain into disregarding his parents' teachings; and "Cain loved Satan more than God," and he entered into a secret combination with Satan and slew his brother Abel and spent the rest of his life as "a fugitive and a vagabond" in bondage to Satan. (Moses 5:16–37.) The first cigarette, the first drink of alcohol, the first pornographic movie, or the first outburst of profanity may, at first blush, seem like such a harmless form of experimentation. But, as with Cain, if these dispositions are not held in check, Satan will, indeed, lead us ever so carefully into bondage.

Sometimes bondage becomes a collective matter. Throughout the ages there have been the rise and fall of many a nation whose citizens failed to protect their individual agency and ultimately found themselves in bondage. The process of slipping into bondage is generally almost imperceptible. From Old Testament times we recall the days of Jacob when there was a famine "over all the face of the earth," and Jacob, having heard reports of plentiful grain in Egypt, dispatched ten of his sons to Egypt to buy grain unknowingly from their brother Joseph. (See Genesis 41:56–57; 42.) Joseph's brothers actually made two separate trips from the land of Canaan to Egypt in order to procure grain, and "it pleased Pharaoh well" that Joseph had been reunited with his brothers and he importuned them to bring their father and their families to Egypt, assuring them that "the good of all the land of Egypt" would be theirs. (Genesis 43, 44, 45:15–20.)

When his sons returned from Egypt, Jacob (or Israel) was elated to learn that Joseph was still alive and, notwithstanding his age and the arduous demands of a long journey, he declared that he would go to Egypt to see Joseph before he died. (Genesis

45:25–28.) An entourage of "threescore and six," departed from Canaan to Egypt, and when those family members were joined by Joseph, his wife, and sons, Ephraim and Manasseh, there were seventy souls of the house of Israel living in Egypt. (Genesis 46:1–27.) With the passage of time "there arose up a new king over Egypt, which knew not Joseph" (Exodus 1:8), and the children of Israel and their burgeoning posterity gradually fell into Egyptian bondage, their stay there lasting for 430 years (Exodus 12:40).

Deliverance From Bondage

Jehovah appeared in a "burning bush" to Moses, an eighty-year-old shepherd, and called him to deliver the children of Israel from bondage (Exodus 3). Jehovah's patience was amply demonstrated each time Moses went to the Pharaoh to request permission to leave Egypt. To get the Pharaoh's attention, Aaron, Moses' brother, "cast down his rod before Pharaoh, and before his servants, and it became a serpent" (Exodus 7:10). Aaron then held his rod above the "waters of Egypt" and they were turned into blood (Exodus 7:19–25). Successive plagues were sent to soften Pharaoh's heart so that he would let the Israelites go free. The first of the plagues consisted of frogs that "covered the land of Egypt." These were followed by a plague in which "all the dust of the land became lice," and then came "a grievous swarm of flies" which remained until Pharaoh appeared to relent and release the Israelites from bondage. But as soon as the plagues subsided he again hardened his heart (Exodus 8).

Notwithstanding Pharaoh's recalcitrance, his life was spared. The Lord then destroyed all of the Egyptian cattle while leaving the cattle of the children of Israel unharmed. This scourge was followed by an outbreak of boils and blains upon all the Egyptians and their animals. The Lord then caused a mighty hail storm in which hail and ground fire destroyed the crops of flax and barley (Exodus 9). Next came a plague of locusts followed by three days of darkness, but still Pharaoh refused to let the people go (Exodus 10:12–27).

After instructing the Israelites to smear the blood of an unblemished male lamb on the two side posts and the upper door post of their houses, the Lord "smote all the firstborn in the land of Egypt" including children and cattle, but the angel of death passed over the homes of the Israelites who had smeared blood on their doorposts. (Exodus 12:5–7; 29–30.) Finally, Pharaoh agreed to let the children of Israel flee from captivity, but as soon as they departed he once again changed his mind and commanded his armies to pursue the fleeing Israelites. As Moses stretched out his hand over the shore of the Red Sea, the sea divided, allowing the children of Israel to pass through to the other side, whereas the horses and chariots and horsemen in Pharaoh's army were engulfed by the sea and "there remained not so much as one of them" (Exodus 14).

Nephi exhorted us to "liken all scriptures unto us that it might be for our profit and learning" (1 Nephi 19:23). One of the lessons we may perhaps draw from the interaction between Moses and Pharaoh is an awareness of the many times and myriad ways a loving Lord has tried to get our attention in order to change our current course of action. Sometimes we listen, but at other times, like Pharaoh, we ignore the Lord's audio-visual aids at our own peril. One lesson is clear from the various encounters between Pharaoh and Moses: the God of the Old Testament exercised abundant patience and long-suffering. Pharaoh was given numerous opportunities to experience a change of heart, and even when he changed his mind and again hardened his heart Jehovah granted him several "second chances."

We can also learn an important lesson from Moses. When first called by Jehovah to lead the children of Israel from bondage, Moses protested, saying, "Who am I, that I should go unto Pharaoh, and that I should bring forth the children of

Israel out of Egypt?" (Exodus 3:11). Moses then expressed his fears that his own people would not follow him, as he told the Lord, "they will not believe me, nor hearken unto my voice: for they will say, The Lord hath not appeared unto thee" (Exodus 4:1). As a final disclaimer, Moses complained of being woefully inadequate in his communications skills: "O my Lord, I am not eloquent . . . but I am slow of speech, and of a slow tongue" (Exodus 4:10). Given such a faltering start and great lack of self-confidence, it is inspiring to observe Moses' spiritual growth, his increased trust in the Lord, and his growing courage in the service of the Lord as he returned to the Pharaoh again and again demanding that Israel be freed from bondage. Newly called bishops, Primary teachers, home teachers, and visiting teachers can take heart from the example of Moses in that we must first face the Pharaoh before the miracles will occur.

Shortly before the Israelites' departure from Egypt the Lord instituted the Passover, a sacred feast involving the partaking of unleavened bread and eating the flesh of a yearling, male unblemished lamb with bitter herbs. This feast was to be kept throughout generations as a memorial of their deliverance from bondage (Exodus 12:1–18). Fifteen centuries later the Savior participated in the passover with His disciples at which time He instituted the sacrament in *remembrance* of His atoning sacrifice much as the passover had *anticipated* His atonement (see Matthew 26:17–29). All of the rites and rituals contained in the law of Moses pointed to the Savior's atonement. Amulek explained that "this is the whole meaning of the law, every whit pointing to that great and last sacrifice; and that great and last sacrifice will be the Son of God, yea, infinite and eternal" (Alma 34:14).

Moses reminded the children of Israel of God's promise that he would show "mercy unto thousands of them that love me and keep my commandments" (Deuteronomy 5:10). Jehovah's mercy toward Israel is amply demonstrated in the constant cloud by day, the persistent pillar of fire by night (Exodus

13:21–22), and by the daily portions of manna He provided them during their four-decade sojourn in the desert (Exodus 16:13–35). He gave them the Ten Commandments to help them increase their devotion toward Deity, to help them overcome the natural man, and to assist them in living peaceably together (Exodus 20:1–7). A modern-day Apostle has reminded us that "all the commandments of God [are] invitations to blessings" (Dallin H. Oaks, *Pure in Heart* [Salt Lake City: Bookcraft, 1988], p. 123).

Extensive dietary laws and rigorous health codes were mercifully given to protect the physical health and strength of the children of Israel (see Leviticus 7, 10, 12–15, 17–18 and Deuteronomy 12, 14). Even more important were elaborate directions on making various sacrificial offerings, including the sin offering and the trespass offering (see Leviticus 4–8). As mentioned previously, these offerings and sacrifices were made in anticipation of the Atonement, for, as Elder Neal A. Maxwell observed: "Personal sacrifice never was placing an animal on the altar. Instead, it is a willingness to put the animal in us upon the altar and letting it be consumed! Such is the 'sacrifice unto the Lord . . . of a broken heart and a contrite spirit,' (D&C 59:8), a prerequisite to taking up the cross, while giving 'away all [our] sins' in order to know God (Alma 22:18); for the denial of self precedes the full acceptance of Him." (Neal A. Maxwell, "Deny Yourselves of All Ungodliness," *Ensign*, May 1995, p. 68.)

After Alma had been the Lord's instrument in bringing many new souls into the Church, these faithful Saints experienced unrelenting persecution at the hands of the Lamanites, but Alma "exhorted them that they should not be frightened, but that they should remember the Lord their God and he would deliver them. Therefore, they hushed their fears and began to cry unto the Lord that he would soften the hearts of the Lamanites. . . . And it came to pass that the Lord did soften the hearts of the Lamanites." (Mosiah 23:27–29.) Faith is

antithetical to fear, and harboring fear is, in large measure, a refusal to be comforted. When we subdue our fears our faith can
flourish, and it is then that hearts can be softened and deliverance is nigh. We worship a God of perfect love, and "perfect
love casteth out fear" (1 John 4:18).

The Lord's deliverance of the Israelites from Egyptian
bondage was a great act of divine mercy and also a profound
type and shadow of the Lord's infinite power in delivering each
of us from individual bondage when we avail ourselves of the
opportunity to repent of all our sins (1 Nephi 17:25; 19:10;
Alma 29:12; 36:28–29). As Alma the Younger retrieved the
painful memories of his life prior to his conversion, he likened
his deliverance from "the pains of hell" to the deliverance of Israel from Egyptian bondage, emphasizing that "none could deliver them except it was the God of Abraham, and the God of
Isaac, and the God of Jacob" (Alma 36:2, 12–22, 28–29). The
God of Abraham, Isaac, and Jacob is a God of mercy and a God
of justice who is able to deliver us from sin, sadness, and sorrow.

EIGHT

The Gathering of Israel:
An Unrelenting Labor of Love

IN FEW PLACES IS THE LORD'S MERCY AND love more abundantly manifest than in His repetitive prophetic promises throughout the entire Old Testament that in His own due time He will gather scattered Israel home.

After securing the promised land from its previous inhabitants, the Israelites divided the land into twelve portions. Members of the tribe of Levi were not allocated a portion of land because they were distributed throughout all the other tribes in order to perform the outward ordinances prescribed by the law of Moses. Each of the other tribes of Israel, including the descendants of Ephraim and Manasseh—the sons of Joseph—received respective portions of land as their inheritance. (Joshua 14–19.)

Kingdom of Israel and Kingdom of Judah

Following Moses' departure from mortality the Israelites were led by faithful Joshua. After his death they were governed by a long line of judges, including Deborah, Gideon, and Samson. (Judges 4, 6–8, 13–16.) Eventually the time came, during the life of the prophet Samuel, when the Israelites insisted on having a king, as all of their neighboring nations had (1 Samuel 8:5–7). It would seem that keeping up with the Joneses is not a modern phenomenon. The Lord reassured his prophet, Samuel, that "they have not rejected thee, but they have rejected me, that I should not reign over them" (1 Samuel 8:7).

Under the Lord's direction, Samuel anointed Saul to reign as the first king of Israel in about 1095 B.C. (1 Samuel 10). Saul later fell into disfavor for his inability to discern that "obedience is better than sacrifice," and with the passage of time he was succeeded by David, who reigned for forty years (2 Samuel 2; 1 Kings 2:11). David's son Solomon then began his reign as a wise and righteous king who built a holy temple to the Lord (1 Kings 2:45–46; 3:6–8), but eventually he married wives who worshipped false gods, and these wives "turned away his heart . . . and Solomon did evil in the sight of the Lord" (1 Kings 11:1–7). Upon Solomon's death, his son Rehoboam laid claim to his father's throne, but, because of his arrogance and autocratic demeanor, ten of the twelve tribes revolted against him and formed the northern kingdom of Israel under the leadership of Jeroboam. The tribes of Judah and Benjamin elected to follow Rehoboam and formed the kingdom of Judah. (1 Kings 12.)

During the next two centuries the inhabitants of both kingdoms intermittently disregarded their sacred covenants until a young king named Hezekiah began to reign in Judah. In contrast to some of his predecessors, "he did that which was right in the sight of the Lord," and "He trusted in the Lord God of Israel" (2 Kings 18:3, 5). Hezekiah assembled the priesthood bearers together and said: "Hear me, ye Levites, sanctify now yourselves, and sanctify the house of the Lord God of your fathers, and carry forth the filthiness out of the holy place" (2 Chronicles 29:5). He sent letters "throughout all Israel and Judah" saying: "Be not ye like your fathers, and like your brethren, which trespassed against the Lord God . . . but yield yourselves unto the Lord . . . and serve the Lord your God." (2

Chronicles 30:7–8.) Hezekiah enjoyed the encouragement and support of the prophet Isaiah, and "the Lord hearkened to Hezekiah, and healed the people" (2 Chronicles 30:20), and "in their set office they sanctified themselves in holiness" (2 Chronicles 31:18).

One of the promises of the Abrahamic covenant was that Abraham's descendants would possess a promised land. Implicit in the promise was that as long as they kept their covenants they would also keep their land. Despite the repeated warnings from numerous prophets, both the kingdom of Israel and the kingdom of Judah eventually forsook the covenants they had made with Jehovah and lost their claim to the promised land. About 721 B.C. the northern kingdom of Israel was carried away to Assyria (2 Kings 17), and around 587 B.C. most of the inhabitants of the kingdom of Judah were taken captive to Babylon (2 Kings 24–25).

Promised Gathering

The merciful promised gathering of a scattered and rebellious Israel is profound proof of Jehovah's persistent love for his disobedient children. The tenth article of faith declares that "We believe in the literal gathering of Israel and in the restoration of the Ten Tribes." It is well to establish the fact that the gathering of Israel was to be an ongoing process following the restoration of the gospel and the organization of the Church, whereas the restoration of the Ten Tribes will be a millennial event when "the Lord, even the Savior, shall stand in the midst of his people, and shall reign over all flesh. And they who are in the north countries shall come in remembrance before the Lord . . . [and] this is the blessing of the everlasting God upon the tribes of Israel." (D&C 133:25–34. See Bruce R. McConkie, *The Millennial Messiah* [Salt Lake City: Deseret Book, 1990], pp. 319–29.)

In Section 110 of the Doctrine and Covenants, the Prophet

Joseph recorded that as he and Oliver Cowdery were in the Kirtland Temple several heavenly messengers appeared to them to convey important keys. Among them was Moses, who committed to them "the keys of the gathering of Israel from the four parts of the earth, *and* the leading of the ten tribes from the land of the north" (D&C 110:11; emphasis added).

Old Testament prophets repeated the Lord's promises that though His children would be scattered as a consequence of their sins, His love for them was infinite, and though many years would pass away, He would not forget them, but would gather them as the Good Shepherd gathers His scattered sheep. Long before they had even possessed the promised land, Moses forewarned the children of Israel that "the Lord shall scatter you among the nations, and ye shall be left few in number among the heathen, whither the Lord shall lead you" (Deuteronomy 4:27). Isaiah prophesied that "the Lord shall set his hand again the second time to recover the remnant of his people. . . . and shall assemble the outcasts of Israel, and gather together the dispersed of Judah from the four corners of the earth." (Isaiah 11:11–12; see also 2 Nephi 6.)

With the passage of time the promise was repeated: "ye shall be gathered one by one, O ye children of Israel" (Isaiah 27:12); "I will bring thy seed from the east, and gather thee from the west; I will say to the north, Give up; and to the south, Keep not back: bring my sons from far, and my daughters from the ends of the earth" (Isaiah 43:5–6). The Lord promised a wayward Israel: "thou shalt not be forgotten of me. I have blotted out, as a thick cloud, thy transgressions, and, as a cloud, thy sins: return unto me; for I have redeemed thee." (Isaiah 44:21–22.)

With poetic eloquence the Lord spoke through Isaiah with the allegorical imagery of a mother's love for her newborn babe: "Can a woman forget her sucking child, that she should not have compassion on the son of her womb? yea, they may forget, yet will I not forget thee. Behold, I have graven thee upon the palms of my hands." (Isaiah 49:15–16.) Jehovah's merciful love for his children is eternal and everlasting.

Through Jeremiah the Lord reaffirmed the gathering process, in which he declared: "I will take you one of a city, and two of a family, and I will bring you to Zion" (Jeremiah 3:14). "I will bring them again into their land that I gave unto their fathers. Behold, I will send many fishers . . . and they shall fish them; and . . . for many hunters, and they shall hunt them from every mountain, and from every hill, and out of the holes of the rocks" (Jeremiah 16:15–16). "Is there any thing too hard for me? . . . Behold, I will gather them out of all countries, whither I have driven them" (Jeremiah 32:27, 37; see also Jeremiah 23:3).

As the Lord's mouthpiece, the prophet Ezekiel continued declaring the prophetic promises to the house of Israel: "I will . . . gather you out of the countries wherein ye are scattered" (Ezekiel 20:34). He then admonished those who have already come into the fold of the Good Shepherd to assist in the gathering process: "Woe be to the shepherds of Israel that do feed themselves! should not the shepherds feed the flocks? . . . my flock was scattered upon all the face of the earth, and none did search or seek after them." (Ezekiel 34:2–6.) Once again the promise is given that "I will bring them out from the people, and gather them from the countries" (Ezekiel 34:13), with the supernal promise: "And I will put my spirit within you, and cause you to walk in my statutes" (Ezekiel 36:27).

The prophet Hosea foresaw that "God will cast them away, because they did not hearken unto him: and they shall be wanderers among the nations" (Hosea 9:17), but he also foretold of the time when the Lord "will say to them which were not my people, Thou art my people; and they shall say, Thou art my God" (Hosea 2:23).

Amos also proclaimed that the Lord "will sift the house of Israel among all nations" (Amos 9:9), and this prophecy was reiterated through Zechariah: "I will sow them among the people: and they shall remember me in far countries" (Zechariah 10:9).

Near the close of his earthly ministry, the Savior of the world overlooked the city of Jerusalem and uttered that immortal poignant plea: "O Jerusalem, Jerusalem . . . how often would I have gathered thy children together, even as a hen gathereth her chickens under her wings, and ye would not!" (Matthew 23:37.) He alluded to a panoramic gathering that far transcended the boundaries of His three-year ministry. He was recalling his divine yearnings as Jehovah, who had sought to gather the scattered children of Israel on many other previous occasions, but they resisted his efforts.

The Gathering Today

In these latter days the Lord has revealed that "there are many yet on the earth. . . who are only kept from the truth because they know not where to find it" (D&C 123:12). He has reminded us that each of us has been called "to bring to pass the gathering of [His] elect," for, said the Lord, "mine elect hear my voice, and harden not their hearts" (D&C 29:7). He challenges each of us to open our mouths in sharing the gospel with others (D&C 33:8–10), declaring that "with some I am not well pleased, for they will not open their mouths, but they hide the talent which I have given unto them, because of the fear of man" (D&C 60:2).

The Lord asks priesthood holders a penetrating question inherent in the Abrahamic covenant and the oath and covenant of the priesthood: "Wherefore, I the Lord ask you this question—unto what were ye ordained? To preach the gospel by the Spirit, even the Comforter which was sent forth to teach the truth." (D&C 50:13–14.) Recalling the counsel revealed to Ezekiel that we are to be "watchman unto the house of Israel" (Ezekiel 33:6–7), the Lord reminds us in our day that "it becometh every man who hath been warned to warn his neighbor. Therefore, they are left without excuse, and their sins are upon their own heads." (D&C 88:81–82.)

Each of us who has claimed the blessings of the Abrahamic covenant must now accept the responsibilities and obligations of that covenant in sharing the gospel with others, because the covenant the Father renewed with us is "not for [our] sakes only, but for the sake of the whole world" (D&C 84:48). Sharing the gospel is an act of mercy enabling others to claim the blessings of forgiveness through baptism and the right to have the continual companionship of the Holy Ghost. The blessings inherent in the priesthood and in the ordinances of the temple are meant to be available to all those who qualify, but alas, there are many who know not where to claim these blessings. Sharing the gospel is an act of justice that ensures that no one will be excluded from participating in the saving and exalting ordinances of the gospel unless it be by their own choice. Sharing the gospel with others is also an act of mercy in providing them with an opportunity once again to be clean and eventually to qualify for entrance into the celestial kingdom and the presence of God.

The Prophet Joseph Smith declared: "Love is one of the chief characteristics of Deity, and ought to be manifested by those who aspire to be the sons of God. A man filled with the love of God, is not content with blessing his family alone, but ranges through the whole world, anxious to bless the whole human race." (*Teachings of the Prophet Joseph Smith*, p. 174.) President David O. McKay's admonition, "Every member a missionary," is a succinct summary of the exhortations of the ancient prophets of Israel and a succinct summary of the modern revelations in this dispensation (Conference Report, April, 1959, pp. 121–22). When we accept this solemn duty the Lord gives us the reassuring promise that "whoso receiveth you, there I will be also, for . . . I will be on your right hand and on your left, and my Spirit shall be in your hearts, and mine angels round about you, to bear you up" (D&C 84:88). We are neither isolated nor alone in this great and merciful, marvelous work of gathering our Heavenly Father's children home, "And thus we see the great call of diligence of men to labor in the vineyards of the Lord" (Alma 28:14).

In a divine proclamation in the latter days the Lord declared: "I, the Lord, am well pleased, speaking unto the church collectively and not individually" (D&C 1:30). The gathering of Israel is "a marvelous work and a wonder," especially when it includes each of us and the members of our families, but if I am not worthy to partake personally of the blessings of the Abrahamic covenant and the blessings of the house of the Lord, then I have not become part of the gathering. If any of us feel excluded from the gathering process the Lord reminds us through his prophets that "thou shalt not be forgotten of me" (Isaiah 44:21), "I have graven thee upon the palms of my hands" (Isaiah 49:16). And to those who listen to the devil's discouraging words that they have sinned beyond the bounds of repentance the Lord gives the reminders that "I, the Lord, forgive sins, and am merciful unto those who confess their sins with humble hearts" (D&C 61:2), and "as often as my people repent will I forgive them their trespasses against me" (Mosiah 26:30).

The ongoing gathering of all of our Heavenly Father's children is evidence of the justice and sense of fairness and also the mercy and love of the Father and of His beloved Son, who extend the universal invitation: "Come unto Christ, and be perfected in him, and deny yourselves of all ungodliness; and if ye shall deny yourselves of all ungodliness, and love God with all your might, mind and strength, then is his grace sufficient for you, that by his grace ye may be perfect in Christ; and if by the grace of God ye are perfect in Christ, ye can in nowise deny the power of God" (Moroni 10:32).

Jehovah of the Old Testament is "the faithful God, which keepeth covenant and mercy with them that love him and keep his commandments to a thousand generations" (Deuteronomy 7:9). He is Jesus Christ of the New Testament, whose infinite mercy was demonstrated by His willingness to die for our sins, causing Ammon to ask, "Who could have supposed that our God would have been so merciful as to have snatched us from our awful, sinful, and polluted state?" (Alma 26:17). After we ourselves have been snatched from our polluted state, it is incumbent upon us to assist in the process of providing this same blessing to others through sharing the gospel with them. President Spencer W. Kimball explained that "the Lord has placed, in a very natural way within our circle of friends, many of those thousands he intends to bring into the Church." (Spencer W. Kimball, "Put Your Hands to the Plow," Seminar for New Mission Presidents, June 22, 1979.)

Through the Apostle James the Lord extended the comforting promise "that he which converteth the sinner from the error of his way shall save a soul from death, and shall hide a multitude of sins" (James 5:20). The Lord promised further: "I will forgive you of your sins with this commandment—that you remain steadfast in your minds in solemnity and the spirit of prayer, in bearing testimony to all the world of those things which are communicated unto you" (D&C 84:61). May each of us claim the promise of having our sins forgiven through sharing with others the gospel of the God of all comfort.

Israel, Israel, God Is Calling

Israel, Israel, God is speaking.
Hear your great Deliv'rer's voice!
Now a glorious morn is breaking
For the people of his choice.
Come to Zion, come to Zion,
And within her walls rejoice.
Come to Zion, come to Zion,
And within her walls rejoice.

Israel, angels are descending
From celestial worlds on high,

And to man their pow'r extending,
That the Saints may home-ward fly.
Come to Zion, come to Zion,
For your coming Lord is nigh.
Come to Zion, come to Zion,
For your coming Lord is nigh.

(Richard Smyth, *Hymns*, no. 7.)

NINE

The Light of the World

WHEN THE GODS "ORGANIZED AND FORMED THE heavens and the earth," the earth was covered with darkness, so "they (the Gods) said: Let there be light; and there was light" (Abraham 4:1–2; see also Genesis 1:1–3). Light and darkness typify an opposition in all things inherent in the great plan of happiness (see 2 Nephi 2:11), and it is significant that in the very first creative period darkness was dispelled and the light was divided from the darkness (Abraham 4:4; Genesis 1:4). The second creative period involved dividing the waters under the expanse of heaven from those above the expanse, and during the third period the dry land was divided from the waters and the earth was prepared to bring forth grass, herbs, and fruit trees. In the fourth period of the Creation "the Gods organized the two great lights, the greater light to rule the day, and the lesser light to rule the night," and the other stars were set in the heavens. The fifth period involved the creation of fishes and fowls and all other forms of animal life. The Gods had now created a hospitable physical environment suitable for sustaining the crowning jewel of the Creation—the human family. (Abraham 4:5–31; Genesis

1:5–31.) Without first providing light, the subsequent creative phases would have been for naught.

Jesus Christ was one of the Gods involved in the process of creation, as recorded in the Gospel of John:

"In the beginning was the Word, and the Word was with God, and the Word was God.

"The same was in the beginning with God.

"All things were made by him; and without him was not any thing made that was made.

"In him was life; and the life was the light of men.

"And the light shineth in darkness; and the darkness comprehended it not . . .

"And the Word was made flesh, and dwelt among us, (and we beheld his glory, the glory as of the only begotten of the Father,) full of grace and truth." (John 1:1–5, 14.)

Not only did Jesus Christ come to earth to teach the word of truth, but also He *was* the Word "full of grace and truth."

The Light of the World

Addressing audiences as varied as Pharisees and disciples, ancient Nephites and Saints of the latter days, the Savior has testified "I am the light of the world: he that followeth me shall not walk in darkness, but shall have the light of life" (John 8:12; see also John 9:5; 3 Nephi 11:11; D&C 14:9). Jesus Christ is "The light and the Redeemer of the world; the Spirit of truth, who came into the world, because the world was made by him, and in him was the life of men and the light of men" (D&C 93:9). As the sun dispels the darkness of the night and sustains life on earth, so the Son of God is "the light and the life of the world" dispelling darkness in the hearts and minds of all mankind, and leading those who would follow him to eternal life. (3 Nephi 9:18; D&C 11:28; 93:9.)

A century and a half before these events actually occurred Abinadi testified "of things to come as though they had already come." With succinct certitude he eloquently declared that Jesus Christ "is the light and the life of the world; yea, a light that is endless, that can never be darkened; yea, and also a life which is endless, that there can be no more death" (Mosiah 16:6, 9). His endless light can reach any recess of a darkened mind or any chamber of a darkened heart anywhere in this vast universe—His light is infinite and unquenchable.

The Light of Christ

In the prologue to his record of the Savior's earthly ministry, John described Jesus Christ as "the true Light, which lighteth every man that cometh into the world" (John 1:9). It is a profound truth that the Savior not only provided mankind with an opportunity to bask in the light of His teachings and His example, but He also infused each member of the human family with His light. Mormon reaffirmed that "the Spirit of Christ is given to every man, that he may know good from evil;" and he exhorted us to "search diligently in the light of Christ that ye may know good from evil; and if ye will lay hold upon every good thing, and condemn it not, ye certainly will be a child of Christ" (Moroni 7:16, 19). Latter-day revelation provides yet another witness that this Spirit "enlighteneth every man through the world, that hearkeneth to the voice of the Spirit" (D&C 84:46; see also D&C 93:2).

Recognizing the infusion of light in every person born upon the earth, the First Presidency declared: "The great religious leaders of the world such as Mohammed, Confucius, and the Reformers, as well as philosophers including Socrates, Plato, and others, received a portion of God's light. Moral truths were given to them by God to enlighten whole nations and to bring a higher level of understanding to individuals.

"The Hebrew prophets prepared the way for the coming of Jesus Christ, the promised Messiah, who should provide salvation for all mankind who believe in the gospel." ("Statement of

the First Presidency Regarding God's Love for All Mankind,"
February 15, 1978.)

President James E. Faust has further stated: "We believe that
all righteous people have the potential to receive inspiration
from God. The many great masterpieces of music, art, poetry,
and other creations of beauty testify to this. Handel's glorious
oratorio *The Messiah* is proof of this. Michelangelo's statues of
the *Pieta, Moses,* and *David* also testify of this. Surely the poet
William Wordsworth was inspired when he wrote "Odes: Inti-
mations of Immortality from Recollections of Early Childhood."
The same is true of the inventors who have been inspired to
bring us all of the marvelous inventions of our time." (James E.
Faust, "Personal Epiphanies," Transcript of CES Fireside for
College-Age Young Adults, January 7, 1996, p. 4.)

To the list of those whose lives reflect the light of Christ
would belong the late Mother Teresa, who dedicated her entire
life to comforting those in need of comfort. When invited to
speak on various occasions, including her acceptance of the
Nobel Prize in December of 1979, it was common for her to repeat the prayer of St. Francis of Assisi, another person whose
life evidenced the light within:

> Lord, make me a channel of Thy peace, that,
> where there is hatred, I may bring love;
> where there is wrong, I may bring the spirit of forgiveness;
> where there is discord, I may bring harmony;
> where there is error, I may bring truth;
> where there is doubt, I may bring faith;
> where there is despair, I may bring hope;
> where there are shadows, I may bring light;
> where there is sadness, I may bring joy.
>
> Lord, grant that I may seek rather to comfort than to be
>   comforted;
> to understand than to be understood;

to love than to be loved;
for it is by forgetting self that one finds;
it is by forgiving that one is forgiven;
it is by dying that one awakens to eternal life.

(Navin Chawla, *Mother Teresa: The Authorized Biography*
[Shaftesbury, Dorset: Element Books, Inc., 1992], pp. xviii, 101,
186, 211–12.)

Referring to a precept taught by the Prophet Joseph, President Faust affirmed: "We believe the Spirit of God can come to all men and women. This is in distinction to the gift of the Holy Ghost. Administrations of the Holy Ghost are limited without receiving the gift of the Holy Ghost." (Op. cit. See *Teachings of the Prophet Joseph Smith*, p. 199.) Sometimes, in our efforts to teach the necessity of receiving the essential ordinances of the gospel, we overlook the importance of acquiring godly attributes that are also a prerequisite for entering into the presence of God.

Every child, regardless of humble circumstances or evil environment, is born into this world with the light of Christ and "every spirit of man was innocent in the beginning" (D&C 93:38). Therefore, the Lord warns us "that wicked one cometh and taketh away light and truth, through disobedience, from the children of men, and because of the tradition of their fathers. But I have commanded you to bring up your children in light and truth." (D&C 93:39–40.)

Ye Are the Light of the World

The God of all comfort expects His children to comfort one another after they have personally partaken of His comfort (2 Corinthians 1:3–4; see also Mosiah 18:8–9). So it is with the diffusion of light throughout the world. The Lord revealed to the Prophet Joseph that "the light which shineth, which giveth you light, is through him who enlighteneth your eyes, which is the same light that quickeneth your understanding; Which light proceedeth forth from the presence of God to fill the immensity of space" (D&C 88:11–12). Notwithstanding the fact that Jesus Christ is "the true light that lighteth every man that cometh into the world" (D&C 93:2), there are many of our Father's children who live their lives in the shadows cast by the prince of darkness. For many, the light within them, though not completely extinct, has grown very dim. Just as plants and trees need light to facilitate the photosynthesis necessary for their survival, the children of men need light to survive, and sometimes survival depends for a time upon borrowed light from parents, neighbors, friends, home teachers, seminary teachers, visiting teachers, bishops, or full-time missionaries.

A loving Shepherd, who would gather all his sheep, taught His disciples: "Ye are the light of the world. A city that is set on an hill cannot be hid. Neither do men light a candle, and put it under a bushel, but on a candlestick; and it giveth light unto all that are in the house. Let your light so shine before men, that they may see your good works, and glorify your Father which is in heaven." (Matthew 5:14–16; 3 Nephi 12:14–16.)

For some individuals, letting their light shine before men can sometimes be a bit challenging in view of the fact that we have also been counseled to be humble, and meek and lowly of heart, and not to do our "alms before men" nor let our "left hand know what [our] right hand doeth" (Matthew 5:1–4; 3 Nephi 13:1–4). Samuel Johnson wryly suggested that when you have a house guest who is continually recounting his own virtues, it may be wise to count the silverware just before he leaves. How then can we allow other people to see our good works so that we might be a comforting source of light to them?

The Apostle Peter provided excellent counsel to the Saints of his day to "be ready always to give an answer to every man that asketh you a reason of the hope that is in you" (1 Peter 3:15). Sister Geney and Sister Alder of the England London

South Mission were walking down one of the streets in Greater London and were surprisingly accosted by an older, dignified gentlemen who said to them: "I want to know what you have." Had the man been much younger and had he been dressed in scruffy attire, these two sisters might have feared that they were being audited prior to being mugged, but this distinguished gentleman continued: "I would like to know why each of you is so radiant and cheerful." These two sisters, according to Peter's counsel, radiated the hope that was within them. A teaching appointment was made, and this gentleman was given an opportunity to receive a systematic answer to his question.

The Savior taught a very important principle regarding how we can let our light shine before others: "The light of the body is the eye; if therefore thine eye be single to the glory of God, thy whole body shall be full of light" (JST Matthew 6:22; Luke 11:34; 3 Nephi 13:22). Evidence of abiding by gospel principles should be apparent in our very countenance. While preaching to the Saints in the city of Zarahemla, Alma asked them a series of forty-one soul-searching questions, including the following: "Have ye spiritually been born of God? Have ye received his image in your countenances?" (Alma 5:14, 19.)

Several years ago Sister Condie and I toured the Spain Barcelona Mission with President and Sister Jesse Judd. In one of the zone conferences all of the missionaries were bright-eyed and obviously committed to building the kingdom, but we noticed one fairly new elder seated near the aisle of the third row of chairs whose countenance virtually glowed. We asked President Judd to tell us a little about that elder. He said: "That is Elder Wilcox. He is a very fine missionary whose father just passed away a short time ago."

After the meeting I felt impressed to take this fine elder into an adjacent room where I could privately provide some comfort to him. I commended him for his devotion in remaining in the mission field after his father's death, and I told him he would feel his father's spirit through the veil from time to time. He replied: "I know. I have already felt him near to me on several occasions."

A year passed and we had another opportunity to tour this same mission again. Once more we met Elder Wilcox, whose mission was now drawing to a close, and to our surprise he had maintained that same radiance we had observed eighteen months previously. This time President Judd informed us that there had been another death in the Wilcox family. Here was a young man who had been through the Refiner's fire. The dross had been removed from his life, and he had claimed the Lord's promise that "if your eye be single to my glory, your whole bodies shall be filled with light, and there shall be no darkness in you" (D&C 88:67). Eyes single to the glory of God are able to penetrate the darkness of death, discouragement, and despair and behold the glimmering lights of the City of God, which lie not so far beyond this mortal sphere.

Radiating the Light

It was my great privilege and blessing to be associated with Sister Karen B. Morgan, who recently passed away after a long and valiant battle with cancer. Her husband had also passed away from cancer a few years previously, so it became necessary for her to return to work to help support her family. She found employment as a secretary to various of the Brethren in the Church Administration Building. Sister Morgan was extremely competent, but in addition to her excellent secretarial skills she provided a ray of sunshine in the lives of all who knew her and worked with her. Stake presidents and mission presidents invariably commented on how cheerfully and courteously they were treated whenever they telephoned Church headquarters.

There would be many women who could be understandably downtrodden after being widowed with a young family to care for, but such was not the case with Karen. She always had an ebullient, cheerful spirit, reflecting her faith in the living God and the promises of the life hereafter. She and her husband and children were sealed for time and for all eternity, and she claimed the blessings of that assurance. Her radiant smile, her sense of humor, and her spirituality blessed us all. Because Sister Morgan had responsibility for confidential information, she was instructed to select a three-letter password for her computer to assure that no one else had access to this information. Although it was only a short time since her husband had suddenly passed away, Karen selected JOY as her password. A couple of years later she was instructed to select a new password consisting of four letters. This time she selected HOPE. Then, not long after her cancer had been detected and the prognosis was guarded and uncertain, she was asked to select still another new password, this time consisting of seven letters. This spiritual giant, filled with light, selected BLESSED. She was a light to the world shining to the end of her earthly probation.

When it comes to radiating the light of Christ, some people act as though this light were generated by batteries, so they are very conservative in keeping their radiance to a minimum lest their batteries run low. But the scriptures are very clear that "he that receiveth light, and continueth in God, receiveth more light; and that light groweth brighter and brighter until the perfect day" (D&C 50:24). As a non-physicist, I do not comprehend exactly how laser beams operate, but it is informative to know that LASER is an acronymn for Light Amplification by Stimulated Emission of Radiation. One means of increasing the intensity of a laser beam is to transmit a beam of light through a series of reflecting mirrors that amplify and focus the light into a very narrow or coherent beam. (Frank J. Blatt, "Masers and Lasers," in *Modern Physics* [New York: McGraw-Hill, Inc., 1992], pp. 191–201.) It is always an inspiring sight to survey the congregation during a stake conference and to observe the number of faithful Saints who radiate a Christ-like countenance and seem to reflect and amplify the light within each other as they meet. Sometimes the greater the number of wrinkles and the whiter the hair, the greater the glow, and, of course, pure little children always radiate light through their innocent eyes.

Teaching with Power and Authority

Some time ago, while Sister Condie and I were touring the England Leeds Mission, we were discussing with the missionaries the indispensability of teaching by the Spirit and of emulating the examples of Alma and Ammon and Aaron in teaching with "power and authority of God" (Alma 17:3). I selected a few scriptural examples of great missionaries who taught with power and authority, but I yearned for a real live here-and-now demonstration. My eye caught Sister Ferguson, a young sister missionary from Belfast, Northern Ireland. I know her father, who is the stake president in Belfast. He and Sister Ferguson have five beautiful daughters, three of whom were born with hearing impairments, and this sister missionary seated before me was one of them. She and her companion are experts in British sign language and are specialists in teaching investigators who are hearing impaired.

Inspired by something I had seen Elder Lynn A. Mickelsen do at the Missionary Training Center in Provo, I invited Sister Ferguson to tell us of Joseph Smith's First Vision in sign language. With considerable animation she depicted the religious fervor and contention during Joseph's youth. We could readily discern from her gestures when young Joseph was studying the Bible, and that he was reading from James chapter one verse five. She vividly described with her hands how Joseph went into the woods to pray, and how he initially wrestled with the powers of darkness. And then the miracle happened: the agitation ceased, and with the index finger of her left hand representing young Joseph kneeling in prayer, she raised her right arm high above her head and slowly lowered her arm with two extended fingers of her right hand pointing heavenward, representing the Father and the Son. The "power and authority" of her teaching was not just in her *hands*, but also in her eyes, and in her radiant countenance with partially opened mouth as she "beheld" in awe the Father and the Son reverently descending to speak to Joseph Smith. That day the missionaries saw first-hand how one can teach with the power and authority of God.

A Light in Darkness

As we walk the streets of some of the great cities of the world it is abundantly clear that there are many people who have darkened countenances with furrowed brows, reflecting countless compromises with conscience. Their faces seem to epitomize the Savior's observation that "if thine eye be evil, thy whole body shall be full of darkness. If therefore the light that is in thee be darkness, how great is that darkness!" (Matthew 6:23; Luke 11:34; 3 Nephi 13:23.)

Two men whose lives were characterized by darkness were King Lamoni and his father. When Ammon first encountered Lamoni, the king was unaware of the great plan of happiness, but through Ammon's disarming ability as a shepherd he endeared himself to the king and gained his trust (Alma 17:20–39; 18:1–23). He taught King Lamoni the gospel, beginning with the creation of the world and Adam and the fall of man, and also telling of the great plan of redemption from sin and from death (Alma 18:24–39). Ammon, having prepared himself through much prayer and fasting and having searched the scriptures diligently, taught with "power and authority of God" (Alma 17:2–3) so that King Lamoni "believed all his words. And he began to cry unto the Lord, saying: O Lord, have mercy . . . And now when he had said this, he fell unto the earth, as if he were dead" (Alma 18:42).

Although the king was comatose "for the space of two days and two nights," and his loved ones began to mourn his loss, "this was what Ammon desired, for he knew that king Lamoni

was under the power of God; he knew that the dark veil of unbelief was being cast away from his mind, and the light which
did light up his mind, which was the light of the glory of God,
which was a marvelous light of his goodness—yea, this light
had infused such joy into his soul, the cloud of darkness having
been dispelled, and that the light of everlasting life was lit up in
his soul, yea, he knew that this had overcome his natural frame,
and he was carried away in God." (Alma 18:43; 19:6.)

After his soul had been infused with light, King Lamoni desired that Ammon accompany him to the land of Nephi to
share the gospel with his father. While en route they met Lamoni's father "who was king over all the land," and to Lamoni's
astonishment, when his father heard of Lamoni's conversion he
became so angry that he commanded Lamoni to "slay Ammon
with the sword." When Lamoni refused his father's command,
his father sought to slay his own son, but Ammon boldly inter-
vened and called him to repentance. The king then turned on
Ammon and sought to slay him, but Ammon "smote his arm
that he could not use it," and "he began to plead with Ammon
that he would spare his life." (Alma 20:1–21.) It seems that
some people are more impressed with visual aids than with the
spoken word.

Ammon prevailed upon the humbled king to release his
brethren from prison, and eventually Aaron "was led by the
Spirit to the land of Nephi" to the father of King Lamoni. Following the pattern whereby Ammon had taught Lamoni,
Aaron began to teach Lamoni's father of the creation and of the
plan of redemption and of the atonement of Christ. The king
asked Aaron: "What shall I do that I may have this eternal life
of which thou hast spoken? Yea, what shall I do that I may be
born of God, having this wicked spirit rooted out of my breast,
and receive his Spirit, that I may be filled with joy . . . ?" (Alma
22:5–15.) Aaron exhorted him to repent of his sins and to "bow
down before God, and call on his name in faith." Then, with
simple faith, devoid of eloquence, the king cried mightily: "O

God, Aaron hath told me that there is a God; and if there is a God, and if thou art God, wilt thou make thyself known unto me, and I will give away all my sins to know thee . . ." (Alma 22:16–18).

This is the price which each of us must pay; we must give away all our sins if we are to know the Father and the Son. We can then claim the Lord's latter-day promise: "It shall come to pass that every soul who forsaketh his sins and cometh unto me, and calleth on my name, and obeyeth my voice, and keepeth my commandments, shall see my face and know that I am; and that I am the true light that lighteth every man that cometh into the world" (D&C 93:1–2).

The father of Lamoni had an experience similar to that of his son. When his mind became infused with the light of the gospel, his body collapsed as if all of his spiritual circuit breakers had been overloaded, so Aaron "put forth his hand and raised the king from the earth" (Alma 22:18–22). The king then began to teach his family and his servants "insomuch that his whole household were converted unto the Lord" (Alma 22:23).

Although the physical reactions to the conversion process are seldom as dramatic as those experienced by Lamoni and his father, the process of casting away "the dark veil of unbelief" and dispelling "the cloud of darkness" by "the light of everlasting life" is replicated hundreds of thousands of times throughout the world as individuals embrace the restored gospel in their lives and participate in the sacred ordinances essential to exaltation.

Our spirituality may be likened to a dimmer switch in a theater or concert hall. To alert the patrons that the performance is about to begin, the lights are gradually dimmed in order to allow people time to find their seats before the auditorium becomes completely darkened. Suddenly one is aware that the hall is very dark indeed. So it is in our personal lives. At first we may feel that our souls are "full of light," but with each off-color story, or sporadic outburst of profanity, or fleeting lustful thought, or moment of unbridled anger, or occasional expression of hatred, or sharing of malicious gossip, or criticism of the Lord's anointed servants, or desecration of the Sabbath, or cutting corners on our tithes and offerings, or with any other act of deceit or dishonesty the light in our lives begins to dim. Any one of the aforementioned acts may cause an almost imperceptible dimming, but the cumulative impact over time does begin to become noticeable, and if we do not repent of these deeds, "from [us] shall be taken even the light which [we have] received" (D&C 1:33) and our "whole body shall be full of darkness" (Matthew 6:23; Luke 11:34; 3 Nephi 13:23).

The Apostle James wrote that "whosoever shall keep the whole law, and yet offend in one point, he is guilty of all" (James 2:10). James conveys the notion that any one sin can rob us of the light just about as well as any other sin. It seems to be part of human nature for each of us to assume that our particular sins are really minor misdemeanors, whereas the sins of others are egregious. Whether one profanes the name of Deity or robs a bank, "from him shall be taken even the light which he has received" (D&C 1:33).

Conversely, every time we lighten the burdens of others through a timely home teaching visit, or a hospital visit, or each time we immerse ourselves in the scriptures and drink deeply from each verse, and each time we plead with our Father in Heaven in prayer and express our gratitude for our countless blessings, and each time we couple our prayer with fasting, and each time we attend the temple worthily, and each time we are engaged in fruitful family history research, and every time we hold a baby or read to a little child, or we pay a sincere compliment to someone who needs a little comfort, and each time we praise a teen-ager and refrain from criticism, and each time we cheerfully accept an assignment to help clean the chapel and the surrounding grounds, and each time we resist an invitation to watch a sleazy movie or video, and each time we defend a friend who is being maligned, and each time we share the gospel with a friend, and each time we tell the truth even when it is difficult—each time the light in our lives begins to increase, because "he that doeth truth cometh to the light" (John 3:21), "and he that receiveth light, and continueth in God, receiveth more light; and that light groweth brighter and brighter until the perfect day" (D&C 50:24). The Prophet Joseph received a revelation that summarizes well the indispensability of the Light of the world in our lives: "The glory of God is intelligence, or, in other words, light and truth. Light and truth forsake that evil one." (D&C 93:36–37.)

Near the close of his earthly ministry the Savior told his disciples: "Yet a little while is the light with you. Walk while ye have the light, lest darkness come upon you. . . . While ye have light, believe in the light, that ye may be the children of light" (John 12:35–36; see also Ephesians 5:8; I Thessalonians 5:5). May each of us become children of light and generously share our light with others.

The Lord Is My Light

The Lord is my light; then why should I fear?
By day and by night his presence is near.
He is my salvation from sorrow and sin;
This blessed assurance the Spirit doth bring.

The Lord is my light; He is my joy and my song.
By day and by night he leads, he leads me along.

The Lord is my light; tho clouds may arise,
Faith, stronger than sight, looks up thru the skies
Where Jesus forever in glory doth reign.
Then how can I ever in darkness remain?

The Lord is my light; the Lord is my strength.
I know in his might I'll conquer at length.

My weakness in mercy he covers with pow'r,
And, walking by faith, I am blest ev'ry hour.

The Lord is my light, my all and in all.
There is in his sight no darkness at all.
He is my Redeemer, my Savior, and King.
With Saints and with angels his praises I'll sing.

James Nicholson (*Hymns*, No. 89.)

TEN

More Holiness Give Me

IN A REVELATION GIVEN JUST THREE MONTHS after the Church was organized in this dispensation, the Lord invited Emma Smith to "make a selection of sacred hymns," for, said the Lord, "my soul delighteth in the song of the heart; yea, the song of the righteous is a prayer unto me" (D&C 25:11–12). Although the contents of our hymn books have changed considerably throughout the years, the general principle guiding the inclusion and publication of hymns has remained the same: the songs of the righteous are to be prayers unto the Lord.

One such sacred prayer set to music is "More Holiness Give Me" by Philip Paul Bliss (1838–1876), who also composed the hymns "Should You Feel Inclined to Censure" and "Brightly Beams Our Father's Mercy" which are included in our current hymn book. The sacred lyrics of "More Holiness Give Me" capture well the life-long process of striving to become like Jesus Christ. This hymn poignantly describes the Savior's service, suffering, sorrow, and grief, and also reflects our own supplication to become more like Him as we experience joy in His service and hope in His word, and as we strive to become pure and free from earthstains through our repentance and his atoning sacrifice for our sins.

Although the title of this moving hymn implores the Lord to *give* us holiness, the acquisition of holiness requires great personal effort inasmuch as "it is by grace that we are saved, *after* all we can do" (2 Nephi 25:23; emphasis added). We gain holiness in much the same way that we acquire the attributes described by President Hugh B. Brown as he wrote: "We ask for strength, and God gives us difficulties which make us strong. We pray for wisdom, and God sends us problems, the solution of which develops wisdom. We plead for prosperity, and God gives us brain and brawn to work with. We plead for courage, and God gives us dangers to overcome. We ask for favors—God gives us opportunities. This is the answer." (Hugh B. Brown, *Eternal Quest* [Salt Lake City: Bookcraft, 1956], pp. 79–80.)

The experiences, testing, and trials leading to holiness may vary from one individual to another. For some, holiness is acquired while pulling a handcart across the plains in a snow storm. For others, holiness may be found after countless prayerful days spent at the bedside of a suffering loved one. Still others acquire holiness after a lifetime of selfless, anonymous service to others. Yet another group of individuals become holy as they freely forgive those who have offended them and humble themselves to ask forgiveness from those whom they have offended.

Prior to His departure from the ancient inhabitants of the Western Hemisphere, the Savior asked them: "What manner of men ought ye to be?" Lest any should doubt the standard He had established, He answered his own query: "Verily I say unto you, even as I am" (3 Nephi 27:27). If we are to become like Him, then we too must become holy as the Lord is holy, for Enoch learned through direct revelation that "Man of Holiness" is His name. (Moses 7:35.) The admonition to become holy is neither a fleeting suggestion nor an unrealistic requirement; rather it is a commandment with a promise: "I am able to make you holy, and your sins are forgiven you" (D&C 60:7).

More Strivings Within

Several years ago my wife and I were shocked to learn that two of our very dear friends, who had given every indication of having a stable marriage, had filed for divorce. Not wishing to meddle in their decision but intent on doing what we could to help, we had a long discussion with the husband about his relationship with his wife. "I just cannot take it any longer," he said. "When business is good and money is abundant, she's easy to live with. But when business is bad and we have to cut back, she is unbearable." Several times during our conversation he said, "I'm tired of fighting and I'm tired of trying."

Every bishop can recall those happy occasions when a less-active couple or new converts have reconciled their differences, repented of their sins, and been sealed in the temple. On rare occasions there are some who, after tasting the delicious fruits of the gospel, nevertheless return to their previous way of life, saying, "We just got tired of trying to fight the temptation to drink, or smoke, or stay morally clean." Paul's counsel to the Corinthians is very appropriate to those who sometimes think that they, and they alone, are the only ones in the world to be subjected to temptation. Said Paul: "There hath no temptation taken you but such as is common to man: but God is faithful, who will not suffer you to be tempted above that ye are able; but will with the temptation also make a way to escape, that ye may be able to bear it" (1 Corinthians 10:13). In short, all temptations are common to everyone, and the Lord will provide the means for our escape if we wish to escape.

Perhaps continual striving within is the means of escape. To the Hebrews Paul wrote: "Ye have not yet resisted unto blood, striving against sin" (Hebrews 12:4). Whenever we may feel like giving up in our strivings against sin, we should realize the active, supportive role that the Holy Ghost can play in our lives if we will be receptive to His promptings. As mentioned earlier, the Comforter *entices* us, *strives* with us, and *persuades* us to do

right (Mosiah 3:19; 2 Nephi 26:11; Ether 4:11). The implica-
tion seems clear that as long as we exert more strivings within,
the Holy Ghost will strengthen our strivings to become more
like the Savior each day, not just striving to resist temptation
per se. The Prophet Joseph Smith taught: "If a man stands and
opposes the world of sin, he may expect to have all wicked and
corrupt spirits arrayed against him. But it will be but a little season, and all these afflictions will be turned away from us, inasmuch as we are faithful, and are not overcome by these evils."
(*Teachings of the Prophet Joseph Smith*, p. 259.)

The fact that Enos prayed all day and night "in mighty
prayer and supplication" was evidence to the Lord of his sincere, inward strivings, and thus he received the promise that his
sins and guilt were swept away. Each of us, no doubt, would also
wish to have our sins swept away, but when we continue to wal-
low in unworthiness and fail to strive to change our present
condition, Satan will assuredly try to discourage us to the point
of giving up. Thus we must follow the example of Enos, and also
of Nephi, who exclaimed: "Awake my soul! No longer droop in
sin. Rejoice, O my heart, and give place no more for the enemy
of my soul." Then, with an even greater resolve he implored the
Lord: "Wilt thou make me that I may shake at the appearance
of sin?" (2 Nephi 4:28, 31.)

More Patience in Suffering

One of the first questions posed by atheists, agnostics, and
cynics in defending their skeptical views of religion and theol-
ogy is: If there is a God, why does he allow so much suffering in
the world? In their minds, the ubiquitousness of suffering is an
indication that there either is no God or that he does not really
care about his children. Of course, nothing could be further removed from the truth. An understanding of the eternal gift of
moral agency helps us realize that because of the very nature of
the gift, some people will unwisely misuse their agency in in-

flicting misery upon others. God allows suffering because he allows people to fully exercise their moral agency for good or ill—but not without accountability.

To ask "Why does God allow suffering?" is not entirely unlike asking the question "Why does God permit fire to burn down buildings and kill innocent victims?" Or, "Why does God allow floods to destroy homes and farms and livestock and human life?" Fire is neither intrinsically good nor bad. When properly controlled, fire can be used for many useful purposes, not the least of which is providing heating for homes and for cooking meals. Water, when kept within proper channels, literally sustains life throughout the plant and animal kingdoms. Like fire, water can be used to purify and to cleanse. And, like water and fire, suffering can also purify us and sanctify us and bring us closer to our Heavenly Father. Sometimes our suffering is seemingly extended and appears to intensify because we, like Jacob of old, refuse to be comforted as we become impatient in suffering.

At such times we should recall the comforting counsel of Elder James E. Faust cited at the beginning of this book: "Out of the refiner's fire can come a glorious deliverance. It can be a noble and lasting rebirth. The price to become acquainted with God will have been paid. There can come a sacred peace. There will be a reawakening of dormant, inner resources. A comfortable cloak of righteousness will be drawn around us to protect us and to keep us warm spiritually. Self-pity will vanish as our blessings are counted. ("The Refiner's Fire," *Ensign*, May 1979, p. 57.)

An extension of the cultivation of hope and faith is the nurturing of patience, for, said the Savior, "In your patience possess ye your souls" (Luke 21:19). Sometimes it is not our immediate circumstances that enslave us so much as our self-imposed impatience that keeps us in bondage. We can accept long-suffering as a godly virtue, but we prefer to experience it in short episodes of hours or days rather than months and years.

The Prophet Joseph's physical and psychological suffering in the Liberty Jail was eased considerably as the Lord tenderly spoke those patience-engendering words to him: "My son, peace be unto thy soul; thine adversity and thine afflictions shall be but a small moment; and then, if thou endure it well, God shall exalt thee on high" (D&C 121:7–8).

In Peter's prescribed process of becoming partakers of the divine nature, patience maintains a prominent position among the godly virtues: "Add to your faith virtue; and to virtue knowledge; and to knowledge temperance; and to temperance patience; and to patience godliness; and to godliness brotherly kindness; and to brotherly kindness charity" (2 Peter 1:5–7). It may be well, during our impatient moments, to put our lives in perspective by comparing our eternal progress to Enoch, who was 430 years old when he was finally translated (D&C 107:49).

More Sorrow for Sin

One of the first doctrines the Savior taught the ancient Nephites was that the law of Moses was now fulfilled and that he would no longer accept their blood sacrifices and burnt offerings, and that they would now be required to offer a sacrifice of "a broken heart and a contrite spirit" (3 Nephi 9:17–20). Paul explained that "godly sorrow worketh repentance to salvation" (2 Corinthians 7:10), and unless and until we truly sorrow for our sins, even to the point of a broken heart, we will not experience the mighty change of heart required of those who become the spiritually begotten sons and daughters of Christ (Mosiah 5:7).

Mormon understood this principle well as he witnessed the downfall of the wicked Nephite nation and observed their "lamentation and their mourning." At first his "heart did rejoice," but, unfortunately, his joy was short-lived because, upon closer inspection, he realized "their sorrowing was not unto repentance, because of the goodness of God; but it was rather the sorrowing of the damned, because the Lord would not always suffer them to take happiness in sin." (Mormon 2:12–13.)

One of Satan's strategies for trying to detour us permanently from the path of righteousness is to make us believe that we are so unworthy it is impossible to find our way back. Sorrow for sin must be kept within an eternal perspective. We must never lose sight of the fact that "men are that they might have joy" (2 Nephi 2:25). Sorrow for sin is a means to an end. The goal of our mortal life and our eternal life is to experience joy and happiness, but we cannot seek "for happiness in doing iniquity" (Helaman 13:38), because "wickedness never was happiness" (Alma 41:10). We must pass through the sorrow for sin in order to achieve true joy.

Alma the younger, King Lamoni and his father, and Zeezrom shared much in common in their respective conversions. Each of them not only felt sorrow for sin, and great emotional turmoil and anguish, but every one of them also experienced dramatic physical manifestations as well. After the angel appeared to Alma he was literally paralyzed for three days until he regained the use of his limbs (Mosiah 27:11–29; Alma 36:8–24). In addition to his paralysis Alma was "racked with eternal torment" (Mosiah 27:29; Alma 36:17), and then after pleading for mercy and relying upon the atonement of Christ, he "could remember [his] pains no more" (Alma 36:19). His previous life of "seeking to destroy the Church of God" (Alma 36:6; Mosiah 27:11) apparently involved no suffering at all. In fact, there may be some indication that his rebellion in concert with the four sons of Mosiah was seen by them as a great source of excitement in life. The physical, spiritual, emotional, and mental suffering Alma was caused to experience was part of the cleansing process brought about through godly sorrow for sin which "worketh repentance unto salvation."

Both King Lamoni and his father fell unconscious for a time following their conversion process, and Zeezrom, after cleverly

trying to outsmart Amulek and Alma as they taught him doctrinal truths, became acutely ill with "a burning fever, which was
caused by the great tribulations of his mind on account of his
wickedness" (Alma 11:20–46; 15:1–3). After Zeezrom had confessed his belief "in the redemption of Christ" Alma healed him
by the power of the priesthood, and he was then baptized and
began "from that time forth to preach unto the people" (Alma
15:6–12). For both Alma and Zeezrom repentance had been an
extremely painful process, but their suffering and sorrow for sin
was but for a moment, whereas their suffering for unrepented
sins would have been eternal.

More Faith in My Savior

The year of 1997 will long be remembered as a time of spiritual regeneration as we recalled throughout the year the "Faith
in Every Footstep" of our courageous pioneer forebears who, in
many cases, left nearly all they had in terms of material possessions in order to gather to Zion. Those overseeing the com-
memorative activities throughout the year wisely recognized
the contributions of modern-day pioneers in addition to those
who crossed the plains. Particularly moving was the construc-
tion of a handcart in Siberia which was pulled across the frozen
terrain of the erstwhile Soviet Union and was air freighted to
New York and then on to Salt Lake City, where it was trans-
ported to the final stretch of the pioneer trail so that it could be
pulled into the valley. It was rewarding to observe that the
Saints in Russia have identified with and claimed the pioneer
heritage as their own. Though the sacrifices of Siberians are
qualitatively different than those of the pioneers of a hundred
and fifty years ago, the sacrifices of these modern pioneers are
nevertheless evidence of great faith in the Savior and His kingdom on earth. The Saints in other countries have also claimed
the blessings of a pioneer heritage in the Church, whether that
heritage consist of an unbroken linkage of six generations or

one's personal conversion just last year. Whenever anyone experiences a mighty change of heart and overcomes the natural man, that person qualifies as a pioneer on the frontier of Zion.

Brother Stephen Robinson has observed that many Saints are quick to believe in Christ, that He lives and that He died for us, but not everyone believes His promises that He can heal us and make us whole. (Stephen Robinson, "Believing Christ," *Ensign*, April, 1992, pp. 5–9.) Christ declared to elders in the early Restoration years: "I am able to make you holy, and your sins are forgiven you" (D&C 60:7). The question for us is: Do we believe him, and if so, are we willing to take the necessary measures to claim his promised blessing? After Enos had prayed day and night for a remission of sins, a voice came to him saying: "Enos, thy sins are forgiven thee, and thou shalt be blessed." Enos then asked: "Lord, how is it done?" And the reassuring answer came: "Because of thy faith in Christ. . . . Thy faith hath made thee whole." (Enos 5, 7, 8.) It is important to keep in mind the fact that it was not the length of his prayer but his faith in Christ that qualified Enos to receive a forgiveness of sins.

Mormon teaches us that "by the ministering of angels, and by every word which proceeded forth out of the mouth of God, men began to exercise faith in Christ; and thus by faith, they did lay hold upon every good thing; and thus it was until the coming of Christ" (Moroni 7:25). Then, when the Savior appeared, he promised: "If ye will have faith in me ye shall have power to do whatsoever thing is expedient in me" (Moroni 7:33).

More Sense of His Care

In his earlier life, when King David was aware of the Lord's watch care over him, he penned the Twenty-third Psalm, which captures well the sense of the Master's care:

"The Lord is my shepherd; I shall not want.

"He maketh me to lie down in green pastures: he leadeth me beside the still waters.

"He restoreth my soul: he leadeth me in the paths of right-eousness for his name's sake.

"Yea, though I walk through the valley of the shadow of death, I will fear no evil: for thou art with me; thy rod and thy staff they comfort me.

"Thou preparest a table before me in the presence of mine enemies: thou anointest my head with oil; my cup runneth over.

"Surely goodness and mercy shall follow me all the days of my life: and I will dwell in the house of the Lord for ever." (Psalm 23.)

It has been said that God exerts a special watch care over little children and newborn lambs. There is another large army who continually experience an acute sense of the Lord's loving watch care. These are his full-time missionaries—elders, sisters and senior couples, preaching the gospel in steaming tropical climes, in frigid Arctic regions, in noisy metropolitan areas, and in remote, dusty villages. As they quietly go about their work—His work—each of them carries the promise that "whoso re-ceiveth you, there I will be also, for I will go before your face. I will be on your right hand and on your left, and my Spirit shall be in your hearts, and mine angels round about you, to bear you up" (D&C 84:88).

More Joy in His Service

While I was affiliated with the Brigham Young University Semester Abroad program in Austria several years ago, we in-vited the distinguished psychiatrist Dr. Viktor Frankl to speak to our group of bright young students. Frankl is the author of *Man's Search for Meaning*, a treatise on the quest for a sense of purpose in life. He rehearsed for our students what he consid-ered to be the major symptoms of an existential vacuum or empty life. These symptoms included aggression, depression, and addiction. He then discussed his solutions to these three respective problems: service, loving someone or something worthwhile, and facing the vicissitudes of life with hope and courage. While discussing service as an antidote to depression, Frankl said, "You Christians [Frankl is Jewish] would do well to follow the Savior's admonition in the New Testament: 'He that findeth his life shall lose it: and he that loseth his life for my sake shall find it'" (Matthew 10:39). Then, speaking as a psychiatrist, he said, "It is very difficult to think about your own problems while you are serving someone else."

Many of us are more than willing to serve when *called* to do so. If the president of the Relief Society calls to ask if we will prepare dinner for a family whose mother is in the hospital, we are very pleased to comply with the request. Or when we are assigned to be the home teacher or visiting teacher to a particular family in need, we gladly strive to meet their needs. Some of us will cheerfully answer the call to serve a mission when we are called to do so. But many of us fall short in terms of self-initiated service, not fully understanding the Lord's admonition that "men should be anxiously engaged in a good cause, and do many things of their own free will, and bring to pass much righteousness" (D&C 58:27).

Some of the greatest service we can render is that which is anonymously given outside the formal organizational structure of the Church, for as King Benjamin declared, "when ye are in the service of your fellow beings ye are only in the service of your God" (Mosiah 2:17). The perpetual problem of nagging wives and hen-pecked husbands can readily be resolved as soon as they come to the realization that washing dishes and changing diapers and earning a living are forms of service to Heavenly Father's other children—their children.

There is an apocryphal account of a stranger walking the streets of a medieval city in Europe. On one of the streets were several workmen engaged in chipping away at roughly hewn stones that had been brought from a quarry. The stranger in town asked the first man what he was doing, to which the workman replied: "Anyone can see I am making stone blocks to build a wall." The stranger approached another workman further down the street and asked what he was doing, to which he replied: "Anyone can see I am building a wall with these blocks." The stranger then approached a third laborer, who seemed to have a special enthusiasm for his work of placing one large block upon another. The stranger extended the same inquiry regarding what the man was doing. The workman stopped, surveyed his work, and then, with glistening eyes and a broad smile exclaimed: "I'm building a cathedral in honor of my God!"

Sometimes the greatest acts of service are performed in remote places by common, ordinary people who will perchance not live long enough to see their seeds of service blossom and flourish. Such is the case with certain missionaries who labor in love in struggling branches in an area where the Church is trying to gain a foothold. After several months in a given area with no apparent measurable success, it is easy to become discouraged, but success must sometimes be measured by survival, not just growth. So it was that the Lord gave His servants the comforting reassurance less than a year and a half after the Church had been restored: "Wherefore, be not weary in well-doing, for ye are laying the foundation of a great work. And out of small things proceedeth that which is great." (D&C 64:33.)

Elder M. Russell Ballard has exhorted us: "Remember, real faith, born of the Spirit, affects every action and our attitudes. When we truly believe, we don't ask 'What do I have to do?' but rather 'What more can I do?' When we truly believe, and when that belief is confirmed upon our souls by the Holy Spirit, faith becomes a causative force in our lives, driving every thought, word, and deed heavenward." (M. Russell Ballard, "Pioneers of the Gospel," Transcript of CES Fireside for College-Age Young Adults, Satellite Broadcast, May 4, 1997, p. 6.)

More Purpose in Prayer

Through years of counseling with people afflicted with anxieties of many different origins, it has struck me as strange that so few of them ever admit to having fervently prayed about the cause of their anxieties, fears, worries, concerns, anger, disappointments, and emotionally upsetting experiences. For those whose unhappiness is lodged largely in impaired interpersonal relationships, Mormon refers to charity as "the pure love of Christ" and he urges "Pray unto the Father with all the energy of heart, that ye may be filled with this love" (Moroni 7:47–48). Prayer is an indispensable means of engendering more tender feelings toward those within our immediate families, of cultivating much greater charity among those with whom we labor, and of reducing untold anxieties about matters which, in an eternal sense, are generally of fleeting importance.

To those whose anxieties are well founded in concerns about chemistry exams, keeping the company solvent, or finding an eternal companion, the prophet Alma admonishes: "counsel with the Lord in all thy doings, and he will direct thee for good (Alma 37:37). In a more recent revelation the Lord exhorts us to "search diligently, pray always, and be believing, and all things shall work together for your good, if ye walk uprightly and remember the covenant wherewith ye have covenanted one with another" (D&C 90:24).

Enos's mighty prayer is a great example of a prayer with a purpose. His initial intent was to gain a forgiveness of sins, and he remained in the attitude of prayer until this purpose was achieved. Interestingly enough, after he had gained the assurance that his sins had been forgiven, he then extended his prayerful concerns to include the welfare of his brethren, the Nephites, and also the Lamanites.

The Savior's prayer in Gethsemane had a great singleness of purpose: "Father, if thou be willing, remove this cup from me: nevertheless not my will, but thine, be done" (Luke 22:42).

Notwithstanding the Divine negation to that plea, the Savior took comfort from the fact that "there appeared an angel unto him from heaven, strengthening him" (Luke 22:43). As we pray with more purpose, may we ever be willing to concede that our purpose should be reconciled to the purposes of the Lord.

I recall being seated in the Salt Lake Tabernacle with a quorum of young priests during general priesthood meeting when President Spencer W. Kimball admonished the members of the Church to offer purposeful prayers focusing upon opening the doors of all the nations of the world for the preaching of the gospel. Said he: "There are many nations where we have not been able to get in, to get visas, or get passports; and it is very important. If we are to fulfill the responsibility given to us by the Lord on the Mount of Olives to go into all the world and preach the gospel to every creature, then we will need to open the doors to these nations . . .

"I hope that every family will hold home evening every Monday night without fail. Missionary work will be one of the strong points that will be brought before it; and the father and the mother and the children in their turns will offer prayers which will be centered around this very important element—that the doors of the nations might be opened to us and then, secondly, that the missionaries, the young men and women of the Church, may be anxious to fill those missions and bring people into the Church." (Spencer W. Kimball, "Fundamental Principles to Ponder and Live," *Ensign*, November 1978, pp. 43–44.)

Twenty years later, Elder L. Tom Perry acknowledged that "we have prayed that the hearts of the leaders of nations would be softened to the proclaiming of the gospel in their lands. We have literally seen doors open to us that have been closed for generations. The Church's message is of joy and salvation and it must be presented to all the inhabitants of the earth." (L. Tom Perry, "Dispensation of the Fulness of Times," Transcript of CES Fireside for College-Age Young Adults, May 5, 1996, p. 6.)

Upon our returning home from our assignment in France a few years ago, our then teenage son, Craig, was asked to speak in sacrament meeting. He related his experiences of going on teaching "splits" with the elders, and he indicated how difficult it was for some people to believe that young Joseph Smith had seen a vision of the Father and the Son in answer to his prayer in the Sacred Grove. Craig then shared the profound counsel drawn from his observations: "If you want to know if Joseph Smith really did see the Father and the Son, just ask God—He was there!"

Joseph Smith had a purpose in prayer, and so must we have. Prayer really can turn the night to day, becoming a reliable avenue of comfort in our hour of need. It is not always necessary for the Great Physician to make house calls if we follow His prescriptions, including a daily dose of spiritual vitamins and a regular regimen of spiritual exercise, and if we consult with Him daily in personal prayer with a purpose.

ELEVEN

More Gratitude
Give Me

MANY SPIRITUAL TRAITS AND VIRTUES ARE GIFTS of God. There seem to be people who are born with great faith and testimonies and "believing blood." Others seem to be blessed with the gift of healing or the gift of tongues. But the acquisition of one particular godly trait is largely up to us, and that trait is gratitude. Heavenly Father can give us countless spiritual gifts and blessings, but it is incumbent upon us to recognize them and to return thanks. The Lord revealed that "in nothing doth man offend God, or against none is his wrath kindled, save those who confess not his hand in all things, and obey not his commandments" (D&C 59:21). It is interesting to observe that ingratitude and disobedience were mentioned in combination as the greatest offenses before God.

In the course of describing different prerequisites associated with obtaining each of the three degrees of glory, the Lord explained that all of his children who do not merit a kingdom of glory "shall return again to their own place, to enjoy that which they are willing to receive, because they were not willing to enjoy that which they might have received. For what doth it profit a man if a gift is bestowed upon him, and he receive not the gift?

Behold, he rejoices not in that which is given unto him, neither rejoices in him who is the giver of the gift." (D&C 88:32–33.)

Captain Moroni is described in the Book of Mormon as "a strong and a mighty man. . . . Yea, a man whose heart did swell with thanksgiving to his God, for the many privileges and blessings which he bestowed upon his people. . . . a man who was firm in the faith of Christ" (Alma 48:11–13). The chronicler of this chapter waxes lofty in his praise of this great military leader, declaring that "if all men had been, and were, and ever would be, like unto Moroni, behold, the very powers of hell would have been shaken forever; yea, the devil would never have power over the hearts of the children of men" (Alma 48:17). It is well to note that high on the list of Moroni's qualities of character was his "thanksgiving to his God."

It is interesting to observe various people's reactions to loss. One couple lost a very large and expensive home in a fire. Their reaction: "We had become so fond of our worldly possessions, we are grateful to be cleansed of the things we had grown too attached to. And we are so grateful we all made it out alive." A woman loses her husband in a sudden automobile accident and exclaims: "I am so grateful for sixteen wonderful years together." A couple lose a little daughter to a rare disease and tearfully respond: "We are so grateful she did not have to suffer long." Another set of parents have a son who was killed while serving his mission. They respond: "He was an obedient son, and we are grateful his mission can continue on the other side of the veil. We are grateful we have been sealed together as a family forever." Yet another man lost a very high-paying position and had to settle for another job with far less status and remuneration. Still his reaction to his new situation was grounded in gratitude. Said he: "In my previous position the company owned my life and I had little time for my wife and family, but now I can spend much more time with them and strengthen our relationship with each other." Gratitude in the midst of adversity makes us superior to our circumstances.

More Trust in the Lord

In the closing chapters of the Book of Mormon, notwithstanding an apparently hopeless situation, Moroni admonished
those of us who would be living in the latter days to trust in the
Lord: "Behold, I say unto you that whoso believeth in Christ,
doubting nothing, whatsoever he shall ask the Father in the
name of Christ it shall be granted him; and this promise is unto
all, even unto the ends of the earth" (Mormon 9:21). Moroni
had lost virtually everything of worldly value, but so strong was
his faith and trust in the Lord that he proclaimed with un-
daunting certitude: "God has not ceased to be a God of miracles" (Mormon 9:15).

The story is told of a farmer who tried with all his heart to
keep the commandments. He refrained from working on the
Sabbath day and he paid a full and honest tithe, observed the
Word of Wisdom in every detail, attended all of his Church
meetings, and served in any position to which he was called.
Yet his family farm was neither particularly productive nor pros-
perous, and there seemed to be the continual battle to make
ends meet.

By contrast, his neighbor generally worked on the Sabbath,
and it was obvious that he infringed upon many of the other
commandments. Still, his crops were consistently more boun-
teous than his God-fearing neighbor's. At last, the righteous
farmer, who was struggling to make a living, could take it no
longer and made an appointment to see the newly called bishop
of the ward. He complained to the bishop of the seeming injustice, as his toil and obedience did not seem to reap the rewards
of his neighbor. After reflecting upon the situation for a moment, this wise bishop replied: "Sam, the Lord doesn't balance
his books in October." A time will come when there will be a
greater harvest than those reaped in the fall of each year. There
will come a judgment that is both merciful and just, and until
then we must trust in the Lord, for "eye hath not seen, nor ear

heard, neither have entered into the heart of man, the things which God hath prepared for them that love him" (1 Corinthians 2:9). This magnificent promise is reserved for those who trust in the Lord. It should also be our goal to lead lives such that the Lord can place his trust in us.

More Pride in His Glory

The Psalmist wrote that "in God we boast all the day long, and praise thy name for ever" (Psalm 44:8). Perhaps it was in this same spirit that Ammon, when chided by Aaron for seemingly boasting of his successful missionary labors, defended his exuberance by replying: "I will not boast of myself, but I will boast of my God, for in his strength I can do all things" (Alma 26:12).

Another enthusiastic missionary, the Apostle Paul, boldly declared: "I am not ashamed of the gospel of Christ: for it is the power of God unto salvation to every one that believeth" (Romans 1:16). Paul was aware that he was not the living water but merely the conduit for that living water as he wrote the Saints in Corinth: "I have planted, Apollos watered; but God gave the increase" (1 Corinthians 3:6). Paul loved his Savior and loved the gospel he confidently proclaimed, but he realized that personal pride was unjustified.

Sometimes, unlike the Apostle Paul, we may mistake timidity for humility, and we may justify our failure to share the gospel with others as humility when, in fact, our feelings are rooted in fear and shame. Of such, the Lord has said: "But with some I am not well pleased, for they will not open their mouths, but they hide the talent which I have given unto them, because of the fear of man. Wo unto such, for mine anger is kindled against them" (D&C 60:2).

President Ezra Taft Benson taught: "In the scriptures there is no such thing as righteous pride. . . . Essentially, pride is a 'my will' rather than 'thy will' approach to life. . . . Pride does not look up to God and care about what is right. It looks sideways to man and argues who is right." (Ezra Taft Benson, *A Witness and a Warning* [Salt Lake City: Deseret Book, 1988], pp. 77–78.)

More Hope in His Word

Nephi admonished us to "press forward with a steadfastness in Christ, having a perfect brightness of hope, and a love of God and of all men" (2 Nephi 31:20). If ever there were a man on earth who reflects a perfect brightness of hope, this man is President Gordon B. Hinckley, who declared: "Well was it said of old, 'Where there is no vision, the people perish' (Proverbs 29:18). There is no place in this work for those who believe only in the gospel of doom and gloom. The gospel is good news. It is a message of triumph. It is a cause to be embraced with enthusiasm" (Gordon B. Hinckley, "Stay the Course—Keep the Faith," *Ensign*, November 1995, p. 71).

As his ministry on earth drew to a close and as he was inscribing the final plates of his sacred record, Moroni focused our minds upon the things that matter most: "Wherefore, there must be faith; and if there must be faith there must also be hope; and if there must be hope there must also be charity. And except ye have charity ye can in nowise be saved in the kingdom of God; neither can ye be saved in the kingdom of God if ye have not faith; neither can ye if ye have no hope." (Moroni 10:20–21.) Faith, hope and charity are not just desirable traits, they are essential to our salvation and our exaltation in the kingdom of God.

Moroni continues by explaining that "if ye have no hope ye must needs be in despair; and despair cometh because of iniquity" (Moroni 10:22). Elder Russell M. Nelson eloquently described how hope is lost and becomes supplanted by despair: "Unrighteous thoughts are the termites of character—and confidence." Then, reflecting his own optimistic and hopeful outlook on life, this modern-day Apostle declared: "Regardless of how desperate things may seem, remember—we can always have hope. Always! The Lord's promise to us is certain: 'He that endureth in faith and doeth my will, the same shall overcome.' [D&C 63:20]. I repeat—there is always hope!" (Russell M. Nelson, "A More Excellent Hope," *Ensign*, February 1997, p. 60.) The Apostle Paul contends that hope is an "anchor of the soul, both sure and stedfast" (Hebrews 6:19).

Elder Neal A. Maxwell observed that hope "keeps us 'anxiously engaged' in good causes even when these appear to be losing causes" (see D&C 58:27). Continuing, he said, "Genuine hope is urgently needed in order to be more loving even as the love of many waxes cold; more merciful, even when misunderstood or misrepresented; more holy, even as the world ripens in iniquity; more courteous and patient in a coarsening and curt world; and more full of heartfelt hope, even when other men's hearts fail them. . . . Genuine hope gives spiritual spunk, including to deserving parents drenched in honest sweat from being 'anxiously engaged' " (Neal A. Maxwell, "Brightness of Hope," *Ensign*, November 1994, p. 36).

An extremely hopeful promise was extended by President Boyd K. Packer to all who have strayed. Said he: "Save for the exception of the very few who defect to perdition, there is no habit, no addiction, no rebellion, no transgression, no apostasy, no crime exempted from the promise of complete forgiveness. That is the promise of the atonement of Christ" (Boyd K. Packer, "The Brilliant Morning of Forgiveness," *Ensign*, November 1995, p. 20). Continuing he said: "And so we pray, and we fast, and we plead, and we implore. We love those who wander, and we never give up hope" (Ibid., p. 21).

More Tears for His Sorrow

The prophet Enoch beheld a vision in which the heavens were weeping "as the rain upon the mountains," prompting Enoch to ask the Lord: "How is it that thou canst weep, seeing thou art holy, and from all eternity to eternity?" (Moses 7:29.) The Lord then explained that all mankind is "the workmanship of mine own hands," and the Lord was grieved because He had "given commandment, that they should love one another, and that they should choose me, their Father; but behold, they are without affection, and they hate their own blood." The ultimate consequence of this spiritual alienation would be that "their sins shall be upon the heads of their fathers; Satan shall be their father, and misery shall be their doom." Then the Lord returned the question to Enoch: "Wherefore should not the heavens weep, seeing these shall suffer?" (Moses 7:33–37.)

If we sincerely desire to become more like Christ, we too must share His tears, not only for our own sins but also for the sins of the world around us. Shortly before departing from this mortal sphere, Nephi confessed that he prayed continually for his people, sharing the heart petal that "mine eyes water my pillow by night, because of them" (2 Nephi 33:3). Nephi had reached the state of personal righteousness in which he was now less concerned with the temptations which so easily beset him earlier in his life, and now his primary concern was for the spiritual welfare of others (see 2 Nephi 4:17–31). Such were also the concerns of the repentant sons of Mosiah, who went forth preaching with great zeal "for they could not bear that any human soul should perish; yea, even the very thought that any soul should endure endless torment did cause them to quake and tremble" (Mosiah 28:3).

The Psalmist promised that "They that sow in tears shall reap in joy" (Psalm 126:5). Those who shed tears for the Savior's sorrows caused by the sins of the world will also shed tears over the sins of their brothers and sisters and children and will care enough not to rest until they have all been safely brought back into the fold.

More Pain at His Grief

Although the atonement of Christ is the central doctrine of the kingdom, as mortals it is impossible for us to comprehend fully this wondrous miracle of forgiveness. In the beginning Adam was taught that his sacrifices unto the Lord were "a similitude of the sacrifice of the Only Begotten of the Father" (Moses 5:7). Jacob also taught that the Lord's command for Abraham to sacrifice Isaac was "a similitude of God and his Only Begotten Son" (Jacob 4:5). Though we may not understand how it is possible for the Son of God to take our sins upon himself, one aspect that is clearly taught is that the Atonement, to be fully efficacious in our lives, requires not only the Savior's sacrifice but also the sacrifice of all our sins (see Alma 22:18).

This requirement to repent of our sins with broken hearts and contrite spirits has been explained by the Savior himself in exquisite detail in this dispensation: "I, God, have suffered these things for all, that they might not suffer if they would repent" (D&C 19:16). We may not be required to atone for the sins of others in Gethsemane, but if we are to become like the Savior of the world we must occasionally spend some time in our personal Gethsemanes of life, and it is then that we can truly experience more pain at His grief.

More Meekness in Trial

I once heard a speech by a noted journalist and social critic who described life in New York City and how one should not always take oneself too seriously. He recounted that he habitually walked down Sixth Avenue each day on his way to his office, and each day he saw a sign in the window of a small store that read: "If you're so smart, why aren't you rich?" For several weeks this question haunted him. "Where is the justice in this world?" he asked himself.

As the weeks wore on, he suddenly arrived at a comforting thought: What is so great about being rich? Wealth carries with it so many responsibilities and burdens. But still there was a kind of gnawing discomfort that a smart fellow like himself should really be making more money than he received each month. The final comforting insight arrived one day when, upon closer introspection, he asked himself the question: "Irving, whoever said you were smart?" He was at peace. Perhaps life was fair after all.

Someone once observed that if the meek are to inherit the earth, they are going to have to be more aggressive! But what a price the aggressive often have to pay in terms of a host of psychosomatic disorders reflective of a mind, body, and spirit not in harmony with each other. Alma counseled his son Helaman to teach the people "to never be weary of good works, but to be meek and lowly in heart; for such shall find rest to their souls" (Alma 37:34). The Lord's antidote for the ongoing trials and tribulations of life is a meek and a lowly heart.

Peter, who knew a good deal about meekness in trial from observing the Savior firsthand, wrote that "the trial of your faith, being much more precious than of gold that perisheth, though it be tried with fire, might be found unto praise and honour and glory at the appearing of Jesus Christ: whom having not seen, ye love" (1 Peter 1:7–8).

Mormon teaches us further regarding the indispensability of meekness: "And the remission of sins bringeth meekness, and lowliness of heart; and because of meekness and lowliness of heart cometh the visitation of the Holy Ghost, which Comforter filleth with hope and perfect love, which love endureth by diligence unto prayer, until the end shall come, when all the saints shall dwell with God" (Moroni 8:26). The Lord himself has given us the following admonition with a promise: "Learn of me, and listen to my words; walk in the meekness of my Spirit, and you shall have peace in me" (D&C 19:23).

More Praise for Relief

A recurrent theme throughout the Book of Mormon is the expression of joy that follows sincere repentance and a mighty change of heart. Alma's poignant conversion story is an apt illustration of the relief from suffering that occurs through the miracle of forgiveness as he exclaimed, "my soul was filled with joy as exceeding as was my pain!" (Alma 36:20).

Following King Benjamin's stirring sermon, his listeners "viewed themselves in their own carnal state" and prayed for the healing power of the Atonement. After so praying, "the Spirit of the Lord came upon them, and they were filled with joy, having received a remission of their sins, and having peace of conscience." (Mosiah 4:2–3.)

Immediately before his physical appearance to the ancient Nephites, the Savior announced from the heavens that fifteen major cities had been destroyed by fire, floods, and earthquakes because of the wickedness of the inhabitants of those cities. With a voice from on high he lovingly invited the Saints to come unto him and to repent or their "dwellings shall become desolate until the time of the fulfilling of the covenant to [their] fathers" (3 Nephi 10:7). Their initial reaction when they heard these words was to "weep and howl again because of the loss of their kindred and friends," but after three days, with the eventual dissipation of darkness and cessation of the earth's trembling, "their mourning was turned into joy, and their lamentations into the praise and thanksgiving unto the Lord Jesus Christ, their Redeemer" (3 Nephi 10:10).

His promise is sure: "I will not leave you comfortless" (John 14:18).

TWELVE

More Purity
Give Me

STRIVING FOR PURITY OF MIND AND BODY IS NOT just a desirable goal but a continual quest, because it is they who are pure in heart who "shall see God" (Matthew 5:8). Both the Apostle John and Mormon articulated clearly that in order to see the Savior we will need to be like Him and become pure "as he is pure" (1 John 3:2–3; Moroni 7:48).

James provided us with wise counsel in acquiring this purity which is needed if we are to enter the presence of the Father and the Son: "Blessed is the man that endureth temptation: for when he is tried, he shall receive the crown of life, which the Lord hath promised to them that love him. Let no man say when he is tempted, I am tempted of God: for God cannot be tempted with evil, neither tempteth he any man: But every man is tempted, when he is drawn away of his own lust, and enticed. Then when lust hath conceived, it bringeth forth sin: and sin, when it is finished, bringeth forth death." (James 1:12–15.)

We should escape from temptations at the first symptom of impending sin, not after a long incubation period during which time lustful or unkind thoughts are given plenty of time to develop into uncontrollable, malignant maturity. Cancerous growths are most easily removed in their infancy. The time to escape temptation is now, as opposed to a little later. Alma also admonished us to "watch and pray continually, that ye may not be tempted above that which ye can bear, and thus be led by the Holy Spirit, becoming humble, meek, submissive, patient, full of love and all long-suffering" (Alma 13:28).

Purity involves more than overt behavior and includes the pledge of the citizens of King Benjamin's kingdom to "have no more disposition to do evil, but to do good continually" (Mosiah 5:2). Once we have lost the disposition to do evil, the seeds of sin have been removed from the seedbed of temptation. Alma very convincingly warned Zeezrom that "our words will condemn us, yea, all our works will condemn us: we shall not be found spotless; and our thoughts will also condemn us" (Alma 12:14). The importance of overcoming a disposition to do evil is reflected in the Sermon on the Mount. The Savior taught a far higher standard than that contained in the law of Moses, which focused primarily upon overt behavior and outward ordinances. The Savior taught that our thoughts and inclinations must be controlled and properly channelled, not just our behavior. Our very disposition to do evil must be overcome. (See Matthew 5–8; 3 Nephi 12–15.)

James addressed some of the same temptations and sins that have recently been addressed by President Hinckley, including the need for members of the Church to avoid profanity and coarse speech. Said James: "If any man among you seem to be religious, and bridleth not his tongue, but deceiveth his own heart, this man's religion is vain. . . . Out of the same mouth proceedeth blessing and cursing. My brethren, these things ought not so to be." (James1:26; 3:10.) Those who are pure practice pure religion as described by James: "Pure religion and undefiled before God and the Father is this, to visit the fatherless and widows in their affliction, and to keep himself unspotted from the world" (James 1:27).

More Strength to O'ercome

A friend of mine recently retired after owning and managing a very successful business for several years. In part because of the pressures of his business he had become enslaved to a bad habit that prevented him from participating in all of the marvelous blessings of the temple. He knew in his heart that his behavior was a violation of the Word of Wisdom, but somehow he seemed to lack the strength to lay aside his bad habits. He had quit several times in the past, but somehow, in a moment of weakness, he picked up the habit where he had left it previously.

Then one cold, wintry day he felt a warm nudge in his heart, and he informed his employees that he would be gone for the remainder of the afternoon. He got into his car and drove into a secluded mountainous area, and there he parked his car and began to hike as far back into a canyon as he could go. When the snow became so deep that he could walk no further, he knelt down behind a big evergreen tree and poured out his soul to his Heavenly Father. He pleaded with God for greater strength to overcome his bad habits, for he longed to become sanctified and purified. As he continued to pray, he promised the Lord that if he could be endowed with greater strength to resist temptations and overcome his habits, he would dedicate his life to the Lord. After he had been on his knees in the cold snow for a very long time, a warm cleansing feeling filled his sin-sick soul, and he felt the healing power of the balm of Gilead.

A few weeks after this experience, the bishop invited my friend into his office to extend a calling to serve as the explorer post adviser. As a hearty outdoorsman, he quickly endeared himself to those eager young men in the ward who also loved the outdoors. His natural talents as a "boys' man" were readily apparent to all of the grateful parents of the youth in the ward. About a year later he received an invitation to meet with the stake president. Filled with apprehension, he and his lovely wife drove to the stake center, where the stake president extended a call for him to serve as the new bishop of the ward. Although completely overwhelmed by the calling, he accepted. He was my bishop, and he sometimes retold the story of his experience on the road to Damascus in order to give others hope that when one really prays in earnest, the Lord will indeed "make a way to escape," as the Apostle Paul promised, and he will give us more strength to o'ercome. Continually reflecting on the two-way promises contained in our covenants with a loving Father in Heaven assists us in our strivings, for, as Elder Henry B. Eyring has said, "Every covenant with God is an opportunity to draw closer to him" (Henry B. Eyring, "Covenants," Transcript of CES Fireside for College-Age Young Adults, Satellite Broadcast, September 6, 1996, p. 2).

More Freedom from Earthstains

In his great intercessory prayer in the upper room, the Savior implored his Father to care for his disciples, adding, "I pray not that thou shouldest take them out of the world, but that thou shouldest keep them from the evil" (John 17:15). Living in the world without becoming part of the world is a perpetual challenge throughout our mortal sojourn on earth. Very early in this dispensation the Lord admonished the Saints to "lay aside the things of this world, and seek for the things of a better" (D&C 25:10). The challenge to live in the world without being of the world was also a problem addressed by Alma as he challenged the Saints in the region of Zarahemla to undergo a mighty change of heart and to "come . . . out from the wicked, and be ye separate, and touch not their unclean things" (Alma 5:57).

During his subsequent ministry to Ammonihah, Alma recounted that during the days of the high priest Melchizedek, men "were called after this holy order, and were sanctified, and their garments were washed white through the blood of the

Lamb." He then proceeded to explain what it means to be sanctified and free from earthstains: "Now they, after being sanctified by the Holy Ghost, having their garments made white, being pure and spotless before God, *could not look upon sin save it were with abhorrence*" (Alma 13:11–12; emphasis added).

Speaking to the youth of Zion, Elder M. Russell Ballard shared his observation that

> our struggle is found in living in a world steeped in sin and spiritual indifference where self-indulgence, dishonesty, and greed seem to be present everywhere. Today's wilderness is one of confusion and conflicting messages. The pioneers had to battle the wilderness of rocky ridges and dusty mountain trails with their faith focused on Zion and the establishment of the Church in the Salt Lake Valley. We too must focus on Zion and put our faith to work in building up the kingdom of God in our wards and branches. We must have the same kind of faith, the same willingness to give our all, even our lives if necessary, to the great cause of The Church of Jesus Christ of Latter-day Saints.
>
> . . . Our journey today is decidedly different from the one taken 150 years ago. We're not fighting wolves and frost bite; we're fighting pornography and drugs. We're not struggling to keep our families alive in a world fraught with the cruelties of nature; we're struggling to keep our values alive in a world that mocks our standards and deems it politically incorrect to live them. We're not working to physically push handcarts over steep mountains and through deep snow drifts; we're working to spiritually push ourselves to overcome discouragement and complacency. (M. Russell Ballard, "Pioneers of the Gospel," Transcript of CES Fireside for College-Age Young Adults, Satellite Broadcast, May 4, 1997, p. 6.)

One of the most pervasive earthstains in today's world is the epidemic of retribution and the inability of various parties to negotiate settlements and reconcile offenses out of court. On the evening news we see families of victims of various crimes who are asked for their reactions to verdicts handed down by the courts of the land, and frequently the responses include comments such as these: "We are bitterly disappointed at the judgment; that doctor should have been ordered to pay at least ten million dollars for his mistake." Or, "How could the judge sentence the drunken driver who killed our son to only five years in prison?" These unforgiving folks will continue to pay a great price for the injustices they perceive, and the costs will be counted in nights of lost sleep, dyspeptic stomachs, migraine headaches, and the loss of peace of mind. The Lord has provided a prescription for peace for each of us: "I say unto you, that ye ought to forgive one another; for he that forgiveth not his brother his trespasses standeth condemned before the Lord; for there remaineth in him the greater sin" (D&C 64:9).

A British clergyman, Michael Pollard, age 62, serving as pastor of the Emmanuel Evangelical Church in Baildon Green, took a trip to Romania with his wife, Jo. They had delivered some humanitarian aid to various Romanians and were returning home to West Yorkshire via Hungary. Late one evening they were viciously attacked by three young Hungarian robbers, who killed the pastor and broke the nose and jaw of Mrs. Pollard. Upon her return home, Jo Pollard held a press conference at which she made the following statement about her attackers:

> I want Christians to reach out for them and pray. I have forgiven them. God loves a person who trusts in him and if they can be brought into his ways he can take away the things they have done wrong.
>
> I don't hate them. Of course, I wish it had not happened, but I cannot undo what happened. I just feel for their families. . . .
>
> This has not challenged my faith, rather it has strengthened it. I know my husband is with Jesus and he is happy . . ." (Paul Wilkinson, "Pastor's widow urges prayers for his killers," *The Times*, London, August 14, 1997, p. 8.)

It has been interesting and inspiring to follow Peter and Linda Biehl's participation in the hearings of South Africa's Truth and Reconciliation Commission (TRC) regarding the possible granting of amnesty to the four black young men who killed the Biehl's daughter, Amy, in 1993. Amy Biehl was twenty-six years old, an idealistic young Fulbright scholar from

Newport Beach, California, who had come to South Africa "to promote democratic change." Four young blacks, who were part of a mob, were convicted of killing Amy in 1993, and each was sentenced to an eighteen-year prison term, respectively. The four young men, Mzikhona Mofemela, Ntobeka Peni, Vusumzi Ntamo, and Mongezi Manqina, were granted the privilege of appearing before the TRC to plead for amnesty for their deeds committed during a time of heightened racial tension and contagious mob violence. In their defense, Peni said: "At the time we were in high spirits. . . . We had no mercy on white people." The four accused men indicated that they were strongly influenced by the Pan Africanist Congress's radical slogan "one settler, one bullet," which they interpreted as granting license to kill all whites.

The interesting part of this saga is that Amy's parents, Peter and Linda, traveled to South Africa to receive the public apologies of the four young blacks, to shake hands with the tearful parents of the young men, and to express their own personal feelings before the TRC. Linda Biehl told the Commission: "We unabashedly support the process which we recognize to be unprecedented in contemporary human history. It is for the community of South Africa to forgive its own. Amnesty is not, clearly, for Linda and Peter Biehl to grant." The Biehls emphatically stated that they were not opposed to amnesty for their daughter's killers. ("Forgiveness," *USA Today*, June 30, 1997, p. 4A; "Killers Apologize for Death of U.S. Student," *USA Today*, July 9, 1997, p. 4A; "S. Africa Amnesty," *USA Today*, July 10, 1997, p. 4A.)

The Doctrine and Covenants articulates the position of the Church regarding the actions of those who violate the laws of the land:

> We believe that the commission of crime should be punished according to the nature of the offense; that murder, treason, robbery, theft, and the breach of the general peace, in all respects, should be punished according to their criminality and their tendency to evil among men, by

the laws of that government in which the offense is committed; and for the public peace and tranquility all men should step forward and use their ability in bringing offenders against good laws to punishment. (D&C 134:8.)

Laws are necessary to maintain peace and order in any society, and "there is a law given, and a punishment affixed" (Alma 42:22), but Linda and Paul Biehl have followed the Savior's admonition to "Love your enemies, bless them that curse you, do good to them that hate you, and pray for them which despitefully use you, and persecute you" (Matthew 5:44). The Biehls are not necessarily soft on crime, especially a crime so heinous as their daughter's brutal murder; however, they have followed the Lord's counsel that "man shall not smite, neither shall he judge; for judgment is mine, saith the Lord, and vengeance is mine" (Mormon 8:20). In modern revelation the Lord repeats the admonition to each of us to "leave judgment alone with me, for it is mine and I will repay. Peace be with you; my blessings continue with you" D&C 82:23). The Biehls will claim an inner peace which the relentless quest for retribution can never provide. They are becoming free from the earthstains of vengeance.

A very pervasive form of earthstain in our lives is the influence of television. In some homes the television is turned on in the early morning hours and is never turned off during the entire day. The Apostle Paul cautioned the Ephesians not to let "fornication, and all uncleanness, or covetousness . . . be once named among you, as becometh saints" (Ephesians 5:3). To those who watch an inordinate amount of television, perhaps the question could be posed: How many murders were committed in your home last week in the room where the television is located? How many times were adultery and fornication and other manner of uncleanness committed in your home—on television? If we are to follow Paul's admonition not to let these things be named among us, then it would seem that a more selective and restrictive video and TV regimen would be in order.

Freedom from earthstains comes from putting a "difference between holy and unholy, between unclean and clean" and then not crossing the line between them (Leviticus 10:10), and this can best be done by following Paul's counsel to "abstain from all appearance of evil" (1 Thessalonians 5:22).

More Longing for Home

Before Alma the Younger experienced the cleansing power of the Atonement, he confessed that "so great had been mine iniquities, that the very thought of coming into the presence of my God did rack my soul with inexpressible horror" (Alma 36:14). In a state of wickedness, the very last thing he desired in life was to be brought into the Lord's presence. However, *after* he had repented of his sins he recounted a vision of "God sitting upon his throne, surrounded with numberless concourses of angels, in the attitude of singing and praising their God; yea, and my soul did long to be there" (Alma 36:22).

Alma's experience and the desires of his heart may well provide us with a useful benchmark in assessing our own current personal worthiness. It would seem that if we are anxious to postpone our entrance into God's presence, we may have postponed some critical areas of needed improvement in our lives. Conversely, on occasion when "a secret something" whispers, "You're a stranger here," and we long to be in the presence of a loving Heavenly Father and his Son, this may be an indication that we are on the right path, notwithstanding our falling short of perfection. (See Eliza R. Snow, "O My Father," *Hymns*, No. 292.)

More Fit for the Kingdom

At the very outset of this dispensation the Lord revealed that "faith, hope, charity and love, with an eye single to the glory of God, qualify [us] for the work" (D&C 4:5). Three months later, but still before the Church was formally organized, the Lord cautioned that "no one can assist in this work except he shall be humble and full of love, having faith, hope, and charity, being temperate in all things, whatsoever shall be entrusted to his care" (D&C 12:8). No mention was made of previous leadership training and administrative experience, but emphasis was given to the indispensability of the traits of godliness so essential to serving with the Spirit.

Becoming more fit for the kingdom generally involves more attention to the details of our lives that either enhance or inhibit our fitness. Sometimes preparation is more important than position. Said the Lord to Hyrum Smith: "Seek not to declare my word, but first seek to obtain my word, and then shall your tongue be loosed; then, if you desire, you shall have my Spirit and my word, yea, the power of God unto the convincing of men" (D&C 11:21). Perhaps Hyrum, like many young missionaries today, was more anxious to reap the rewards of preaching than to invest the time and effort needed to adequately prepare to preach. Fitness in the kingdom involves more than just showing up, and more than just participating.

Bill Walton, former NBA basketball player and previous star for the UCLA Bruins, recalled how excited he was to join Coach John Wooden's team in the fall of 1970. Coach Wooden, affectionately known as the Wizard of Westwood, had coached his teams to seven consecutive national basketball championships between 1967 and 1973 and he finished his career with ten national championships in twelve years. Walton showed up for the first practice session filled with the anticipation of discovering some of Coach Wooden's "strategic secrets." What followed in that first session was somewhat of a surprise:

"Coach Wooden came in, sat down on a stool and had us gather around him," Walton recalls. "He said, 'Gentlemen, today we are going to learn how to tie our shoes properly.'"

At which point, the Wizard demonstrated that, maybe, everything we need to know, we didn't learn *well enough* in kindergarten. He showed his new recruits, step by painstaking step, how to knot their shoelaces so they would never, ever come undone during a game. Then he took off his socks—Walton remembers that Wooden's toenails were not a pretty sight—and showed how to put on sweat socks so they would never, ever bunch up inside the sneakers and cause a blister. Then it was on to the rest of the uniform. . . . The sessions continued with lessons on how to warm up, how to eat and sleep properly. . . .

This wasn't exactly what Walton had in mind about studying at the master's feet, but it made an impression he never forgot. . . .

Wooden was a master of getting his players physically and mentally, technically and tactically ready to perform at a championship level *all the time*. He knew the best way to avoid jittery performances was to eliminate self-doubt and instill confidence that the opponent could do nothing for which his teams had not practiced. (Barry Lorge, "What It Took To Win," *The Wall Street Journal: Advertising Supplement*, March 27, 1997, p. 20.)

To those who would be teachers, the Lord has said, "Seek not to declare my word, but first seek to obtain my word" (D&C 11:21). It is generally more exciting and fulfilling to teach than to laboriously study and prepare, just as Bill Walton thought it was more rewarding to play basketball than to listen to Coach Wooden teach him the basics of tying his shoes. But a promise is given that after we have studied and prepared and obtained the word, "then, if you desire, you shall have my Spirit and my word, yea, the power of God unto the convincing of men" (D&C 11:21), and "if ye receive not the Spirit ye shall not teach" (D&C 42:14). He further exhorts all who would be teachers to "preach the word of truth by the Comforter, in the Spirit of truth" so that "he that preacheth and he that receiveth, understand one another, and both are edified and rejoice together" (D&C 50:17, 22), for "when a man speaketh by the power of the Holy Ghost the power of the Holy Ghost carrieth it unto the hearts of the children of men" (2 Nephi 33:1). President Hinckley has coalesced all of these scriptures into one profound aphorism: "The Holy Ghost is the Testifier of Truth, who can teach men things they cannot teach one another"

(Gordon B. Hinckley, "The Father, Son and Holy Ghost," *Ensign*, November 1986, p. 51). If we would be more fit for the kingdom we would do well to remember that preparation invites the Spirit into our work for the Lord.

Those who would be leaders are reminded that "the rights of the priesthood are inseparably connected with the powers of heaven" and that "no power or influence can or ought to be maintained by virtue of the priesthood, only by persuasion, by long-suffering, by gentleness and meekness, and by love unfeigned; by kindness, and pure knowledge, which shall greatly enlarge the soul without hypocrisy, and without guile" (D&C 121: 36, 41–42). Yes, fitness in the Lord's kingdom is not to be measured by university degrees or by the administrative acumen gained through experience in the world of business. Fitness in the Lord's kingdom requires "the hearts of the children of men. . . . the heart and a willing mind" (D&C 64:22, 34).

More Used Would I Be

The purpose of the various offices and callings and responsibilities within the organization of the Church is "for the perfecting of the saints" (Ephesians 4:12). It may be challenging for a good speaker with great scriptural knowledge to silently serve as an assistant ward clerk while a very humble and shy brother is called to serve on the stake high council. The well-organized, articulate working mother and homemaker may be called to serve in the Primary nursery while her timid neighbor down the street is called to serve as the ward Relief Society president. The ward clerk and the nursery leader may harbor in their hearts the secret desire to be more used in the kingdom. "More used" is often confused with "more visible," and the Lord has forewarned us that those who seek to "gratify [their] pride [or] vain ambition" will not have the privilege of being guided by the Spirit (D&C 121:37). When we keep in mind that the Church is for the perfecting of *all* the Saints, not just current leaders, we immediately realize that the very talented must sometimes learn humility by serving in low-profile positions, while the timid and weak must be strengthened in faith by being called to positions that will stretch their souls and abilities.

Elizabeth Barrett Browning poignantly observed that

> The best men, doing their best,
> Know peradventure least of what they do:
> Men usefullest i' the world are simply used.
> The nail that holds the wood must pierce it first,
> And He alone who wields the hammer sees
> The work advanced by the earliest blow. Take heart.

(Aurora Leigh: A Poem in Nine Books, [London: Smith, Elder & Co., 1890], p. 170.)

President Hinckley reminds us: "There is nothing unimportant about any call in this Church. Every call is important. When we all do our duty working together, the whole Church moves forward in an orderly and wonderful fashion." (*Teachings of Gordon B. Hinckley* [Salt Lake City: Deseret Book, 1997], p. 66.)

While I was serving in a bishopric of a ward with nearly eight hundred members and a high level of activity, it became apparent that we were running out of meaningful callings and positions. We became concerned about extending a call to a very spiritual and energetic couple to serve as the eighth couple on our activities committee. Social activities are very important to any ward, but it is probably not an optimal situation to call sixteen people to plan and implement all of the activities. We prayed and labored long over this challenge of how to find fulfilling callings for every member of a ward with hundreds of faithful and committed Latter-day Saints.

Eventually the answer to our prayers came. We should be anxiously engaged in good causes and do many things of our "own free will" (D&C 58:27). We spoke to the congregation about formal Church callings that generally involve regular meetings and rather specific duties and responsibilities. Next we talked about the responsibilities we have as members of the Church, as a community of Saints, regardless of any official, visible position in the kingdom. We suggested that those who would be "more used" in the kingdom could spend more time in the temple, and could invest more energy in family history research, and visit more neighbors who were aged, lonely, or ill, and visit the hospital more often, and write more letters to missionaries and to those in the armed services. After that sacrament meeting a number of members expressed their gratitude for the new perspective they had gained about their membership and service in the Church.

More Blessed and Holy

Paul admonished the Ephesians to "be renewed in the spirit of your mind; and that ye put on the new man, which after God is created in righteousness and true holiness" (Ephesians 4:23–24). It is interesting how often we refer to various Saints as "good men and women," but seldom, if ever, do we refer to someone as a "holy woman or man." Perhaps in our attempts to avoid the impression of being holier-than-thou, we set our sights on being ethically decent for the most part, but in the process we may fall short of being holy.

The Lord has commanded us in these latter days to "practise virtue and holiness before me continually" (D&C 46:33; 38:24). Indeed, members of the Church are admonished to "manifest before the church . . . that they are worthy of it, that there may be works and faith agreeable to the holy scriptures—walking in holiness before the Lord" (D&C 20:69).

More, Savior, Like Thee

As Mormon describes the attributes of charity, "the pure

love of Christ," he is in reality describing the godly attributes of the Savior himself: "And charity suffereth long, and is kind, and envieth not, and is not puffed up, seeketh not her own, is not easily provoked, thinketh no evil, and rejoiceth not in iniquity but rejoiceth in the truth, beareth all things, believeth all things, hopeth all things, endureth all things" (Moroni 7:45; see also 1 Corinthians 13:4–7).

When Elder Joseph B. Wirthlin was serving as president of the Europe, Africa, British Isles Area of the Church, it was my blessing and pleasure as mission president to have Elder and Sister Wirthlin tour the Austria Vienna Mission. The Wirthlins had been travelling extensively throughout a vast geographical area, so they were just a little weary when we met them at the airport, and then we drove them a considerable distance to the location of our first zone conference with the missionaries in the early afternoon.

Following a four-hour meeting with the missionaries we intended to take Elder and Sister Wirthlin to a restaurant for dinner that evening, but at the conclusion of our meeting Elder Wirthlin asked one of the missionaries if he knew a certain family who had recently moved into this part of the mission. When the missionary said he did know the family and that they lived about an hour away, Elder Wirthlin asked him to call the family to see if we could visit them.

An hour later we were in the living room of a fine Latter-day Saint family who were overwhelmed and delighted that Elder and Sister Wirthlin had come to see them. The Wirthlins had known this family several years previously, and it became apparent during their conversation that the father of the family had been subjected to Church discipline a few years previously. Elder Wirthlin did not want to leave the city without being assured that his friend was making progress toward returning to the Church. After about an hour of gentle yet direct counsel accompanied by the brother's commitment to prepare to return to full fellowship, we left a prayer in that wonderful home and

Elder Wirthlin was then ready to have dinner prior to making our long journey back to the mission home in Vienna. Within a year of that visit, that young father returned into full fellowship in the kingdom. He had responded to the voice of a loving shepherd who sought out his Father's lost sheep. *Charity is kind and rejoiceth not in iniquity but rejoiceth in the truth.*

During this same period of time the restored gospel was starting to percolate throughout the countries of eastern Europe. As the first contact of the Twelve for Europe, Elder Russell M. Nelson often visited these countries, and on one occasion I was invited to accompany him and Elder Hans B. Ringger, a member of the Europe Area Presidency, on a visit to various eastern countries. In one country we had experienced considerable difficulty in retaining the services of an attorney who could represent the Church in various matters concerning legal recognition, acquisition of property, permission to publish materials, and so forth. Eventually we were able to retain the services of a very bright and capable young woman who had received good legal training and seemed to be a person of high integrity. She was not a member of the Church, as is often the case in many countries where the gospel is just beginning to be preached.

We had arranged for Elders Nelson and Ringger to meet with our attorney the morning after our arrival in the country. As we arrived at our hotel, I called the attorney's home to confirm our appointment with her the next morning. To my great dismay she spoke with very slurred speech, and it was abundantly clear that she had had far too much to drink. She explained that she had lost two cases in court that week and was very distraught, but she had remembered the appointment and she would be pleased to meet with us.

The next morning it was evident to everyone present that our lawyer had an Olympic-size hangover. I was excruciatingly embarrassed. What would Elder Nelson think? Here is an Apostle of the Lord Jesus Christ speaking to an attorney who had

been retained to represent the Church and who, on this occasion, looked somewhat like the last twenty minutes of a mis-
spent life. Nevertheless, she was gracious and as pleasant as
could be expected, and, I must admit, she was articulate and ef-
ficient in her processing of details and in reporting progress on
certain matters in question. At the conclusion of our meeting
we shook hands and bade her adieu.

As soon as she left, I apologized profusely to Elder Nelson
for having hired such an attorney to handle some of our legal
affairs in that country. My face was flushed from the embarrass-
ment I felt. This loving Apostle placed his hand gently on my
shoulder and said: "Here she is, unmarried, living alone, and
trying her best to compete in a male-dominated society in a
male-dominated profession. The Savior has a soft spot in his
heart for a young woman like her." *Charity is not easily provoked
and thinketh no evil.*

A couple of years ago I was assigned to a stake conference in
California, and, unbeknown to me, Elder Henry B. Eyring was
scheduled to take the same flight in order to attend another
stake in the same general area. Elder Eyring took his place in
about row seven and I took my seat in the row in front of him.
Just as we were getting buckled up, a little girl about age ten
came down the aisle and spoke to Elder Eyring. "Excuse me,"
she said, "but that window seat is mine." Elder Eyring graciously
arose so she could get over to her window seat. After she was
settled in, I overheard him gently ask: "What's your name?" She
replied: "Sarah." Elder Eyring then said: "Hi, I'm Hal." He then
engaged her in a conversation that was at her level of comprehension but not in the least condescending. Here is a man who
has been a Harvard graduate, Stanford Professor, renowned
business consultant, President of Ricks College, Commissioner
of the Church Educational System, an Apostle of the Lord, and
he introduces himself to a sweet little girl as Hal. *Charity is not
puffed up and seeketh not her own.*

I attended a series of area priesthood leadership training

meetings in Seattle with Elder M. Russell Ballard two years in succession. The first year he was in robust health. The second year the meetings were held shortly after he had undergone extensive open heart surgery. As he stood to address about a hundred stake presidents in the chapel, he said: "Brethren, I hope you'll accept my apologies for coming back two years in a row." He then proceeded to teach by the power and authority of the Spirit, and every one of the brethren in attendance was exquisitely instructed, edified, and inspired. Elder Ballard had been through the Refiner's fire during the weeks prior to that meeting, and he was quickened by the Spirit in the things he taught. After the meeting, one of the stake presidents who had attended the meetings the year before said, "Please tell Elder Ballard it was all right to come back again this year. He wasn't the same Elder Ballard as last year." The president went on to explain that the previous year's instruction had been wonderful, but this year the Spirit had been stronger.

We had a similar experience in our area training meetings in Solihull, England, in which Elder Neal A. Maxwell presided. In the throes of leukemia, and anticipating the forthcoming agony of extensive chemotherapy that lay ahead, Elder Maxwell truly focused upon the things that matter most. Though his physical body was in a weakened condition, it was obvious to all that he had been purified, and his testimony rang with certitude borne of the Spirit. *Charity hopeth all things*.

My wife and I had the blessing of participating in a regional conference in Oregon with Elder Richard G. Scott shortly after his lovely Jeanene had passed away following a long and valiant battle with an extended illness. Although the conference was held in a very large, acoustically sensitive basketball coliseum with several thousand Saints in attendance, when Elder Scott rose to speak a hush came over the audience as the Spirit distilled upon all those present. Elder Scott had recently experienced the pangs of separation and loneliness as his eternal companion had been temporarily taken from him. But he had also been blessed with that comfort that passes human understanding. For over an hour he held those Saints absolutely spell-bound as he, like his Brethren, taught by the Spirit. Notwithstanding the large number of young children in attendance, for more than an hour there was absolute reverence in the coliseum as an Apostle of the Lord testified to the Saints of the truth of the restored gospel and of his sure knowledge of the eternal ordinances of the temple. *Charity beareth all things.*

Elder David B. Haight has been a valiant defender of the faith and a great missionary and a very special witness. Now, after nine decades on earth, his eyesight has been severely dimmed, becoming a considerable inconvenience in his life. But this faithful soul continues to work harder building the kingdom of God than men half his age. In one of the meetings with the General Authorities a few years ago, when Elder Haight's eyesight was beginning to fade, we sang "How Firm a Foundation" as the opening song. We sang the first three verses and closed our hymn books. Elder Haight then asked President Hinckley if we could sing verse seven, to which the President replied affirmatively. So, at Elder Haight's urging we sang:

> The soul that on Jesus hath leaned for repose
> I will not, I cannot, desert to his foes;
> That soul, though all hell should endeavor to shake,
> I'll never, no never, I'll never, no never,
> I'll never, no never, no never forsake!

(Robert Keen, "How Firm a Foundation," *Hymns*, No. 85)

For Elder David Haight, *charity endureth all things.*

I do not wish to be intrusive in the lives of all of the Brethren we sustain as prophets, seers, and revelators, but suffice it to say, from these few vignettes from their lives, each and every one of them has been tried and tested. The trials and tribulations have varied, but each has been in a crucible in which the dross has been removed and they have become special witnesses because they have led special lives. They are not immune from the troubles of either the body or the soul, and their trials and tribulations, disappointments and suffering, have sanctified them. Through the process of becoming holy, and of becoming more like the Savior, they have become acquainted with the God of all comfort, and by so doing they are able to comfort the rest of us even as they have been comforted. They speak "the pleasing word of God, yea, the word which healeth the wounded soul" (Jacob 2:8). They follow the admonition of an apostolic colleague who counseled them and us to comfort others by the same comfort wherewith we ourselves "are comforted of God" (2 Corinthians 1:4).

INDEX